# amerika

Russian Writers View
the United States

D1478337

# amerika

## Russian Writers View
## the United States

### Edited by Mikhail Iossel and Jeff Parker

Dalkey Archive Press

Copyright © 2004 by Dalkey Archive Press

First edition, 2004
All rights reserved

All individual essays collected in this volume are copyrighted by the respective authors and translators and cannot be reproduced without permission.

First Dalkey Archive edition, 2004
All rights reserved

Library of Congress Cataloging-in-Publication Data

Amerika : Russian writers view the United States / edited by Mikhail Iossel and Jeff Parker.— 1st Dalkey Archive ed.
    p. cm.
    ISBN 1-56478-356-1 (acid-free paper)
    1. United States—Foreign public opinion, Russian. 2. Public opinion—Russia (Federation) 3. National characteristics, American. 4. United States—Civilization—1970- 5. United States—Relations—Russia (Federation) 6. Russia (Federation)—Relations—United States. 7. Authors, Russian—Attitudes. 8. Authors, Russian—Travel—United States. I. Iossel, Mikhail. II. Parker, Jeff, 1974-

E183.8.R9A67 2004
973—dc22
                                                                                          2003070082

Partially funded by a grant from the Illinois Arts Council, a state agency.

Dalkey Archive Press books are published by the Center for Book Culture, a nonprofit organization located at Milner Library, Illinois State University.

www.centerforbookculture.org

Printed on permanent/durable acid-free paper and bound in the United States of America.

# Contents

E
1838
.R9
A67
2004

102704-1228 F8

# Introduction

## Mikhail Iossel

America has more people populating it, but Russia exceeds America in the size of its territory by a factor of 2:1. Yet Americans tend to guard their private space with much greater zeal. Those interested in the circumstantial confirmation of this assertion are invited to compare their experiences of a rush-hour subway ride in New York and in Moscow.

In fact, there is no direct equivalent for the American expression *private space* in Russian.

Many more Russians know English than there are Americans who can read or speak Russian.

There are seven more letters in the Cyrillic alphabet, used by the Russians, than there are in the English one. The average Russian's glottal area, then, is inured to producing a greater variety of phonemes than that of the average American. Roughly the same—minuscule—number of Russians and Americans know the meaning of the word *phoneme.*

Russians are much more interested in America, on average, than Americans are in Russia. Americans are inclined to believe this is so because America is so much more interesting than Russia could ever be. Russians are of the opinion that they are just possessed of a much livelier curiosity about the rest of the world than the majority of Americans are. Both points of view are essentially correct.

America is the modern world's success story. Russia provides a horror narrative, a cautionary tale.

America is never too far from the ever-changing epicenter of the average Russian's thoughts. There has never been a time in that hypothetical average Russian's life when America would not be domiciled in his mind. Does one remember the first time one saw the full moon? No. Does one remember the time before one had seen the full moon for the very first time? No. It's the same with America.

Russians still, in a carry-over of a Soviet-era bromide, like to think of themselves as a nation of the world's most avid readers. American bookstores, however, are infinitely more numerous and well-stocked.

Most Russians read pure, unadulterated trash. So do most Americans.

Russians are much poorer than Americans. A much greater percentage of people are poor in Russia. The Russian and American respective definitions of poverty are vastly dissimilar.

America is more diverse, less homogeneous than Russia. There are many more *mini-Americas* in America than there are *mini-Russias* in Russia, if you will. Americans, *en masse,* are quirkier than Russians, because they can afford to be. Many more of them do not have to worry about what they and their children are going to eat for breakfast every morning: they have more spare time on their hands. They are much freer, therefore, to spend their spare time arranging their personal, private space in accordance with their personal ideas of what their lives are all about.

There are, indeed, many *Americas* in America. Sometimes one wonders what it is, exactly, that holds them all together, except the commonality of geography and language—and, to a lesser extent, that of the shared but differently interpreted idea of personal freedom. The twangy country singer who rhymes *Bin Laden* and *forgotten* in his televised performance at the Pentagon represents one America, Harold Bloom discussing Hamlet on the *Charlie Rose Show* on PBS quite a different one.

Americans, one might suggest, are an entity of people living in one place, speaking roughly the same language and bounded by an unspoken agreement to consider themselves an entity of people called Americans.

Americans, on average, are more overtly friendly than Russians are. This is understandable: they live, by and large, in much greater comfort. America, simply put, is a more comfortable place to inhabit. It is a more *sunlit* kind of place. Why, pray tell, would a comfortable and frequently sunlit individual be unfriendly?

Still, regrettably, there are very many unfriendly, mean-spirited assholes (pardon me) in America also.

There are many more deeply religious, genuinely God-fearing people in America than there are in Russia. This, too, is easy to explain: an excess of spare time in one's life inevitably leads one to start searching for the overall meaning of one's existence—and it is only in very rare instances (only when one, fortunately for him, happens to be a person of great intellectual autonomy) that such a search can be conducted without one's constant appellations to the forces of the supernatural.

The average American is shallow and woefully self-involved. So is the average Russian.

Some of the associations conjured up in the average Russian's mind at the mentioning of the word *America* tend to include: Indians (in a well-known Chekhov story, two teenage Russian boys are planning an escape to America in order to fight on the side of the Red Indians); Mark Twain and Jack London (two all-time favorites of many generations of young Russian readers); cowboys, popcorn, Coca-Cola, Madonna, Michael Jordan and Michael Jackson, Shaq Attack; baseball; arrogant superpower; they only respect brute strength and people and nations that can stand up to them; pitiable nation of hamburger-eating, flag-waving meatheads; Brighton Beach (the notorious *Russian* enclave in Brooklyn, a time warp on par with the Galapagos Islands); Russian mafia (Russians can be touching in their belief that *our* Russian mafia can outmafia all comers hands down); John Reed (free-lance journalist, Communist, author of *Ten Days That Shook the World,* known to American movie-going audiences as the central character in Warren Beatty's award-winning 1981 epic, *Reds*) and Dean Read (boyishly good-looking country-pop singer from Colorado, K-Mart cross between Elvis and John Denver, extraordinarily popular in the Soviet Union in the sixties and seventies; claimed to have been stripped of U.S. citizenship for demonstratively washing the U.S. flag in dirty, soapy water in front of the U.S. Embassy in Santiago, Chile; wrote and subsequently published in the ubiquitous Soviet weekly *Ogonyok* [Little Flame] an open letter to Alexandr Solzhenitsyn, castigating the latter for his anticommunist stance; lived in the Soviet Union for a while, later on moved to East Germany, where he went on to forge a lackluster spaghetti-western career and eventually was found dead, floating face-down in a shallow lake not far from Berlin);

Faulkner, Dreiser, Hemingway, Henry Miller, Salinger, Bukowski (plus, as of recently, Pynchon, Roth and Burroughs; contemporary American literature is pretty darn great, no argument there—still, the great nineteenth-century Russian literature was much, much greater!); arrant imperialism, shameless chauvinism, how many little American flags can one stick on one's beat-up car? (it's those with nothing to show in the way of the Great American Dream who are the most patriotic, or jingoistic, of course); *Yankee, Go Home!;* why do you think there're so many more American flags on proud display in a trailer park than on Park Avenue!; deep down, they're just like us; they're well-off, autonomously well-regulated to the point of being able to have elected as their leader not the sharpest knife in the drawer, not the smartest man among them, to put it charitably; they like to talk about themselves too much, the self-infatuated creeps; they smile too much, they show their teeth an awful lot; they are ludicrously obsessed with their health, such hubris, why are they so bent on prolonging their boring lives by a few more years?; even their dead are probably happier than our living; antidepressants galore, virtually in every family, whereas in Russia no one ever gets depressed, apparently, by dint of keeping oneself either drunk or hungover for most of the time; whiskey is a much more treacherous drink than vodka, and that sums up the American national character, come to think of it; they can't drink; single-celled organisms, that's who they are, with absolutely no psychological depth to them!; their women are no match for ours, willfully sexless and coldly aggressive, they're apt to slap you with a lawsuit if you as much as cast a flirtatious glance at them, is it any wonder then that their poor underappreciated, unattractive men keep coming over to Russia in droves to marry our beautiful, feminine, docile Russian women? . . . the gullible fools; they think they're all that; they talk about the most personal of their problems with total strangers, they have no shame; they don't understand the true meaning of the word *friendship;* oh, they're wonderful, moral, hardworking people; effing puritans, Bible-thumpers, self-righteous creeps, almost hounded a perfectly good president out of office for a measly blow job; they have such excellent teeth!; what do they know about real suffering, they're rich rich rich rich rich rich rich . . .

About America, the average Russian knows everything—and nothing.

The Russians pronounce their letter *k* (and they do have one; its corresponding character is called *kah*) in a harder fashion than Americans do theirs; they (the Russians) put more mustard on it. (Toby Keith, the Ford Truck-hawking, never-compromisin', super-tough author of the famous "Angry American" song—"This big dog will fight / When you rattle his cage / And you'll be sorry that you messed with / The U.S. of A. / 'Cause we'll put a boot in your ass / It's the American way!"—may think he's plenty tough indeed, but the puniest of Russian pussies pronounces his last name in a much tougher way than he ever could: *K-k-kif!*) When the Russians say *America,* they pronounce it like this: Ameri*k*a.

The Russian alphabet character *c* corresponds with the Latin *s*. Therefore, when the native speaker of Russian sees the word *America* written in Latin characters, in his non-dormant *immediate* mind—one unencumbered, as it were, by layers of cognitive sophistication—it sounds like this: *Amerisa.*

*Amerisa?* It doesn't make any sense.

*Amerika,* then. With a *k*. The Russianized America. The America that does not require a later-knowledge-based translation into Russian. What can one say about it? That was the question posed to the authors in this volume: What do you think of when you hear the word *Amerika?*

Everything—and nothing.

Amerika.

# amerika

Russian Writers View
the United States

# MISTAKES IN THE GUIDEBOOK

## MIKHAIL AIZENBERG

I began to be asked what I thought of America the morning after my arrival. I answered, "As I see it, America is a country of unlimited possibility." It seemed to me that this was a good joke, but America, obviously, has a different psychological climate. My interrogator began in all seriousness to persuade me that I was a victim of ideological brainwashing. Very likely. With each day, my definition of America became more and more broad and indistinct. Any collective generalization is usually stupid. The more extensive my personal impressions, the more exceptions have stubbornly showed up to undermine the rule. And worst of all are those unsolicited observations so willingly given before your journey: the roads are terrific, the subways are terrible, everybody smiles like an idiot, nobody smokes, and there is an overall lack of spiritual dimension. I don't know. Any of this has to be said carefully and diffidently, stretching "but" as far as possible. Moscow neighborhoods have no reason to envy the asphalt surfaces of New York, where the subway isn't terrible at all, just old. True, one time I got lost there, wandered off my beaten track, and really fell into a whole other world. Debris and dirt. Exotic black people contemplated me from their trash barrels. On their tranquil faces some thoughts could be discerned, but I didn't like them. I remember specifically that no one was smiling.

In general, people smile in moderation, and you see smokers everywhere. I find it difficult to evaluate the level of lack of spirituality, as statistical data are somewhat confusing. In *New York* magazine the listing of art exhibitions takes up five pages of small type. This is, let's admit, not particularly surprising: the western art market is the most grandiose (and was the most underreported) mercantile affair of the twentieth century. But there are also around fifty poetry readings every day. Everybody knows that nobody reads poetry. So why then do poetry publications fill up the shelves on one whole wall in a bookstore? Clearly, it's part of the décor or because

this bookstore is located on the main street in the famous university town
of Ann Arbor, where I passed the greatest part of my time in America.

Back in Moscow I had first read that name forty years earlier on the title page of a book by Nabokov: "Ardis / Ann Arbor." I took in the sound of
these unfamiliar words like a magic spell of cultural incantation. And now,
here I had fallen into the second part of that incantation.

All college towns somewhat resemble one another, like happy families.
(This, by the way, is already a generalization, and generalizations, as we know,
lead us astray.) The glass-paned front doors on many homes are, I confess, one
of my strongest American impressions. The last murder in Ann Arbor was
fifty years ago. During my brief sojourn a terrible scandal erupted, the talk
of the whole town, and the local newspaper slapped it up on the front page.
The coach of the university hockey team, in an inebriated condition, stopped
his car, got out to take a piss, and the police busted him. Community opinion was divided. Many people thought this was an inappropriate exercise of
authority, discrediting our athletic star, our pride. Interesting that even in a
university town, right now only the athletes are celebrities. Here, it's especially
remarkable that sport is a kind of ideology, and I was somewhat intrigued and
discomfited that people could be so unified, and so easily led by entertainers
in colorful caps. Moreover, we watch this show, not trusting our own eyes,
through binoculars. Binoculars? Who foisted these onto us?

"You should use Nabokov's *Pnin* as your guidebook for your time in
Ann Arbor," suggested one experienced New American. I don't think he
had it quite right. When you look through a lens like that, observations
of the subject immediately appear along fascinatingly familiar, gracefully
rollicking, humorous lines, attached to no reality (except that of Nabokov's
prose). Nevertheless. Certain new acquaintances were not able to establish
their own existence beyond that of characters in a book. The plump, emi-
nent scholar of Russian who had dedicated his life to a language he never
got around to learning correctly. A dark-skinned student who quickly fell
asleep somewhere between the fifth and sixth phrase of each of my brilliant
lectures. The gorgeous graduate student Nadia, who seemed to be slathered
in a special, perfumed lotion, with glasses and a straw hat. Or that person

reminiscent of a weasel—a sharp, freckled little face, prickly eyes—who was really just a professor who spun out of a few lines of my favorite poet enough thread for a solid body of academic work. This professor considered all "new" poetry—whatever has been written during the last half-century—a misunderstanding, and he regarded with distaste the sudden interest of his own graduate students in authors who had not yet achieved the exalted and admirable status of being dead.

His graduate students were good. Especially the girls, of course. And not just the plain ones, the bluestockings. Good looks added a special pleasure to the inquisitive diligence of certain girls who stood out from the rest. Let's remember especially the marvelous hair (golden under ash blonde) of Karen, who came onto campus riding a motorcycle and wrote down our Moscow telephone number with a magic marker on her wrist. She's never called, by the way. But in any case, sweet Karen, Stephanie, both Lauras, both Elizabeths, Julia, Susan, Rachel! Always glad to carry on a conversation. About Vaginov—a trap to catch a whole flock of cultural suggestions. About a photograph of Stalin on the windshield of a bus carrying a coffin with the dead Shalamov. About whatever you like. I am confident that you will all become fine Slavic scholars. In your eyes there was so much open, honest attention that nothing else, nothing extraneous, could find room. No outside interest at all, alas. No sly scintillation, no special electricity, no pointed discharges of a kind so familiar you take them for granted, and so, when you have come to live for a while in a different erotic climate, you begin to sense it as a shortage of oxygen.

In this country girls blush if you catch their eye by chance. You have to be careful all the time, as if you were an elementary school teacher, and—God help you!—not disclose your maniacal tendencies. (These tendencies, you understand, will only get worse.) But there are sparks, currents, subtle flashes, disturbing little lightning bolts in the depth of an accidental glance which are essential. Eyes meet, separate, probably forever. Still, you have had the opportunity for an imperceptible shock, and the cardiac jolt lingers, freezing you, until the next glance, corner, day.

. . . The girl turned and *looked* at me. I jumped (this time visibly) and understood that after a month I have grown completely unaccustomed to something like this. But the scene of action has changed: I have come for a day to another university and I am looking at the campus with innocent eyes. A wet path winds around ornamental trees (plane trees? beeches? hornbeams?). She turned again. If she looks a third time, I'll go after her, I'll spit on the honorarium. She looked. I did not spit.

We met the woman who has set up this reading in a Chinese restaurant not far off the main street. It's usually a bad idea to eat before work, and everything that followed corroborated this. Jane (my hostess) immediately started a conversation that was not uninteresting to both of us: whether Conceptualism was dead, or Socialist Art alive, and which exactly was which. The talk was very much to my taste and even lively, leaving no room for unfamiliar culinary impressions. But soon a new participant joined in, and at last, thoughtfully, I applied myself to the shrimp. Were those mushrooms? No, that's what I had in a Thai restaurant. I'm terrible at remembering foods: I have already forgotten what exactly broccoli is, and the name of that edible pine-cone that I was told you eat by tearing off the oily scales and sucking the contents. Artichokes! I have forgotten the taste of fried oysters, king crab, sea urchin doused in sweet soy sauce (served in a little varnished wooden box) and marvelous "nagimi yaki": beef stuffed with green onions and grilled in spiced soy sauce with bean sprouts. I got carried away, just when I shouldn't get carried away.

"We want a perfectly natural environment for these evenings. A live interaction among the students, faculty and visitors, Russian tea and cake and so on," the hostess told me beforehand. I could not quite understand what she had in mind. They quickly sat me and the poet Jim Kates, here filling the role as translator of my poems, on a low, lumpy sofa (the direction of my digestion changed suddenly and the food began to rise) and I was immediately blinded by the glare of tiny floodlights. The room preserved a natural, funereal silence. It was impossible to guess who or how many were present.

Trying to discharge the atmosphere prickling with electricity, I began to joke, treating the darkness to a disarming American smile. This is not my usual style. As far as I could tell, no one was gratified by my treat. Nor did I succeed in changing the tone, and on this jocular wave I began to read my not very hilarious compositions. At about the fourth poem I was drowned out by a lordly knocking on the door. Where I come from, everyone still shudders at a knock like that. Jane dove to the doorway and dove back with a joyful announcement, "Here is our favorite professor Henry Rabinowitz!" I looked at the visage spread out before me and joked, in an attempt to rouse the public one more (and, I swear, the last) time: "Well, he's come just in time to hear a poem about him." The brawny favorite Henry scorned the coat-rack and, settling in the first row, took his time arranging his noisy overcoat on his lap. "Henry, now you'll hear a poem about you," announced Jane in a lecture-room voice. This communication caught the professor's interest, but somehow did not seem to please him, and I broke into a cold sweat. It was too late to retreat, there was nowhere to hide. So I read, after all, a little poem in which a Jewish theme is touched on with what seemed to me accessible humor. In former appearances among any audience, when I read this one, a funny little noise would rush through, reassuring the author. In any other setting, but not here. The silence was even more deadening, from funereal it became otherworldly. The matter had clearly taken an unforeseen idiomatic turn. I surreptitiously looked at the upturned eyes of the professor and understood that they had now written me off for making an ethnic slur.

I think my surname saved me. Softened the blow, so to speak. By the end of the reading (about forty minutes later) the audience had swallowed my little joke. Some questions followed, finally they handed around the promised cake, the guarantee of naturalness . . . The unwilling hero of the evening approached for clarifications: "Does anybody still write poems in Moscow? Do they give readings?" I can understand that he found it hard to believe.

All the same a sensation of terrible awkwardness stayed with me. Something tossed and turned in my soul. It oppressed me, "as does, in retrospection, a blunder we have made, a piece of rudeness we have allowed ourselves, or a threat we have chosen to ignore" (*Pnin,* really).

"Apparently, my joke fell flat?" I asked Jim on the trip back. "Very flat," my friend answered with uncharacteristic sharpness.

*Translated by J. Kates*

# The Ocean: A Journey to San Francisco

## Anatoly Barzakh

Each morning I was freezing. I would wake in a gray mist, not even in a fog, but rather like in a plane descending into a cloud. Surprisingly, if you drive even a short distance away from Sunset, say in the direction of Buena Vista, you find yourself in another city, or at least in other climes. It was there, on the steeply rising slopes of the Buena Vista hill, that I witnessed the meeting of two men: one in a parka and another in shorts. The cold wind was coming in from the ocean, from where we came, while the warm wind came from the direction of downtown, the way we were heading. The thinning mist revealed light, like a 3D film. Neither sunset, nor sunrise, but the wiping of a grimy glass. Even in Berkeley, on the other side of the bay, by 11 or 12 A.M., it was still gray and cold, until swiftly there came warmth and light. Strange. I had seen something like this on an autumn morning in the forest, but in a city? Only when walking in the Berkeley Hills did I realize, suddenly, what was happening. At about seven in the evening, something dark appeared over the ocean, far away from the shore, condensing. The cloud began to widen, to puff up, and then suddenly made its way toward the hills, enveloping everything in a frosty mist that only the rays of tomorrow's high noon would melt. So, this is the ocean. Here lies the source of the strange unquiet that I've been feeling lately. As a dog senses the presence of a wolf, so too my subconscious mind feels the presence of the Other—it is He, the Ocean.

Everything here is permeated by its powerful presence: the weather that changes abruptly from one block to the next, these trees that, seemingly for no reason at all, bend in the same direction, with their shortened branches turned toward the ocean and raised in a defensive gesture; this salty, peeling residue on the skin washed away by the evening shower, and this strange climate that combines cool summers and tropical flora.

Not that I perceive the ocean as an animated being (though perhaps it is no accident that Stanislaw Lem, in his *Solaris,* gave the ocean an intelligence, one beyond the understanding of humans, and not capable of understanding them), but neither can I call it dead, mechanical, like slot machines. One is almost horrified by its power, indifferent to you, to the very fact of your existence, the power that, with rational and cool regularity, fills the horizon with mist and calmly yet swiftly exhales it on the city, the valley, the bay, the hills. As if the Alien, that rhythmically breathing Monster, permeates the air itself and its horror lies not in its suspected malevolence, but in its cold indifference to you, in its total ignorance of your existence.

This sense of awareness of the ocean's presence can only be compared to Descartes's *cogito:* the background is almost more important than the foreground. The thing is that the protruding foreground is nothing more than a plaster cast, décor, a slot machine, while there is nothing more real than this vague, indefinable, alien background. The ocean is an anti-*cogito* of a sort, something that will never become a part of me, but, at the same time, as well as *cogito,* it is ever present.

America, however strange it may sound, is closer to the edge of the world than I expected (it's not called the New World for nothing), having been stuffed with popular secondhand images of a rational, technologically superior civilization. Here, one is overwhelmed by the feeling of a basic lack of groundedness and safety. (How can it be otherwise, if the basis of European culture, that is Descartes's *cogito,* is not just negated, but is turned inside out, is supplanted by the sensation of the Other, the Ocean?) For instance, almost every house in San Francisco is just one or two stories high and is made of light planks of some kind—this is a seismic zone, and nothing can be done about it—and even the magnificent skyscrapers of the downtown cannot silence the hum of anticipation, of the hidden presence of underground shocks, and the same oceanic diffused sense of an indifferent and overwhelming power. Or just take this: a few steps from the university campus there hangs a poster, amusing in its earnestness, warning of the dangerous but possible encounter with a mountain lion. You can ignore it (to your own peril, as the knowledgeable people say), but whether you do or not, the wild is too close to the settled space. The wilderness is real; it constitutes the inescapable background that reminds you that this is not a home, but a fort under siege, not a city, but something else. Of course, the city does not disappear; the city of San Francisco is beautiful, but again as *landscape;* that is, the city's image is not, first and foremost, a sum of its houses, streets, planning, and architecture, but is rather composed from marvelous landscapes, from all these sudden, sharp hills and ravines, wiggly sounds, and green spots of parks, from these "vistas" that are so engaging if viewed from different points, and from the dozing ocean that frames these geological structures.

In other words, even the city that is supposed to shield you from the world—such is its function in Europe, where putting Culture against Nature is, essentially, the same as putting the city against the steppe, the forest, the field—is absorbed, expropriated by the world, by nature, by the ocean: the hills dotted by houses, the bays filled by forests of masts are perhaps prettier than empty hills and bays, but the décor is superficial, it does not bring culture to nature. In opposition with most European cities where the landscape becomes a part of the city, here the city becomes a part of the landscape. Perhaps this is where the unhealthy impulse to proclaim one's victory over nature comes from. As if the grandiose Golden Gate Bridge could really bind the ocean. Moreover, the sense of fragility, danger, mortality that the pompous décor of this galvanized symbol of triumph of reason and will attempts to camouflage, to displace, immediately comes back to the surface: just before the bridge there is a glade and a walk studded with tiles engraved in memory of someone or other. There are even sentimental epitaphs engraved here, and the same can be found on benches: one thinks twice before sitting on them, and before stepping on the memorial tiles.

A similar thing on the Berkeley campus: each graduating class is eager to leave a mark by erecting a bench, a bridge, a bear sculpture; there is even a bench in honor of the university's president who granted self-rule to graduate students. As if memory cannot be contained to libraries and cemeteries. Well, books are perhaps too abstract, they are not things, not *real* things, while cemeteries are excessively functional: they do not convey a firm belief in the existence of other worlds, they lack a separate (cultural) plane. Meaning and memory should be close at hand; and, even better, they should not be kept at a distance by culture or custom. Such distancing is fragile and invites suspicion. Memory should be written into landscape, should become a part of the world (a bench, a bridge, a walk): this is more reliable than erecting a sculpture that has too much culture in it and therefore cannot be depended on. Culture will not save us from the ocean, from the mountain lion, from the earthquake. Culture is décor, appearance, not an immediate experience, not a crutch: therefore Hurst gives the University a sports arena that is an exact copy of one from classical antiquity, and the mayor of San Francisco erects in the city's garden a copy of the famous sculpture of Diana the Hunter, and the church buildings present the whole spectrum of European architectural styles of bygone centuries. Here is the same desire to keep close by, the same inability to distance one's self, the same fear of forgetting and losing, the same doubt in the existence of meaning, of a memory plane: the object is real, the meaning is doubtful.

Take cemeteries: there is one under the freeway coming from the Golden Gate Bridge, a cozy pet cemetery where there are moving inscriptions, mustached bas-reliefs, modest gravestones of unknown cats. Here we see the same passion to materialize memory, even a nameless memory, even the memory that lies beyond the confines of the conscious. I found the cemetery touching, especially because it was not an exclusive memorial ground for the filthy rich, but seems to be an ordinary, customary establishment. At the same time, I felt that here some fundamental law had been violated, and some rules had been ignored, perhaps unjust and cruel rules, but those that set a certain hierarchy. Not a hierarchy of nature, but a hierarchy of the city. The same goes for the blocks of one-story homes, complete with front lawns, almost at the center of San Francisco, whose presence demolishes the "big city"/"small town" hierarchy. I felt the same thing in Berkeley, where a football coach or victory in a sporting event on one hand, and a professor that made a world-class discovery within the walls of his *alma mater* on the other, are equally immortalized: every job well done deserves praise, one achievement is *a priori* no better than another. The triumph of a consistent democracy, in effect, is equal to the destruction of culture, and nowhere is it more evident than when it is seen against the backdrop of the ocean, of the danger that levels any hierarchy. The idiocy of "political correctness," the marginalization of culture, the flourishing of subcultures: all these are not just an expression of attention to the rights of minorities, their right to be different, but consequences of the inherent negation of hierarchy.

America's uniqueness is mostly due, I think, to the all-encompassing and incurable neurosis of its frontier (the New World) existence: the neurosis of marginality, homelessness, of living at the outpost (the cliffs of San Francisco are symbolic in this respect). This neurosis was perhaps contracted by the first settlers who found themselves, often against their own will, in a hostile, dangerous, alien, unpredictable world.

These are not metaphors, but reality. Today's unconquerable hostility of nature: tremendous tornadoes and hurricanes, devastating earthquakes; sharks preying on swimmers not far from straight-laced Washington, D.C.; angry and pitiless grizzly bears in well-kept national parks . . . I believe the shock experienced by Americans on September 11, 2001, is due, in part, to an ever-present subconscious fear, or even an expectation, of a catastrophe that would strike at the very center of the world. It is not the matter of the terrorists or Bin Laden—it is the ocean that casts away the cultural mold that means nothing to it (and perhaps means nothing to those who cannot overthrow its power, as well), even if the mold is the super-skyscraper.

It is not the destruction of a seemingly unshakable foundation, but the elucidation of the primeval, the unconquered, banned to the innermost hiding places, exhausting the anxiety of being. Could it be that the secretly gnawing awareness of this imminent and indifferent danger is the source of both the banal American longing for a standard happy ending, and of the constant balancing on the brink of a catastrophe that is the staple of even the most insignificant blockbusters? And although Sylvester Stallone and Arnold Schwarzenegger, having come through mind-boggling adventures, save the world (the USA, a woman, a child, reputation of the service, etc.), this final "triumph of virtue" fails to do away with the deepening sense of uncertainty, the sense of danger personified by the all-powerful mafia clans, corrupt presidents, judges, and policemen. We can only have faith in a superman, but where can we get one? The miracle of salvation is a mirage, just like any miracle—a story where a happy ending is a must, while the danger threatening *everything* and lurking *everywhere* is real and is experienced in reality. Only, danger comes not from the outside, but—more terrifying— is hiding inside of us, in the place we call soul, where lurks the anti-*cogito* Other, what in Greek was called the messenger, the angel of the ocean.

This fundamental fragility, this existential danger, is the leitmotif of the cinema of Stanley Kubrick. His characters cannot be sure of their own motives and passions. It's not the content of their nightmares that matters, which could well be "European." Instead it is the helpless horror they feel before the uncontrollable, the alien, which surreptitiously breaks through their last defenses and penetrates the holiest of holy places: their self-awareness, their personality, and their psyche. The Other's breathing inside me instills horror: the anti-*cogito* inside myself. Presence turned inside out. I wonder if, in the final count, the above-mentioned marginalization is not propelled by the fear of the Other. Better not to suppress the alien Other, not to contain it. If cornered, it will only get deeper inside us, and in self-preservation it will pose as one of the crowd. Whereas, by giving it freedom, we at least have a chance to control it and, somehow, to tame it.

*Translated by Matvei Yankelevich & Efrem Yankelevich*

# Chelyabinsk-Moscow

## Dmitry Bavilsky

That which is greater than us (a feeling, a city, a country) cannot be described adequately. In fact, any such portrait is the description, not of an object, but of the one describing.

It's a strange affair: in Moscow I have met with unabashed anti-Americanism, far stronger than in the provinces. That is, in the provinces I generally didn't clash with anti-American sentiments at all. The fringe elements don't count.

It is understandable why this is the case: America is closer to Moscow (I myself live in the Urals) in all senses, and not just geographically. Moscow finds itself more dependent on America, even if it is only because it attempts to live and work in the same form and likeness. In Moscow, the willfulness of personal interests is clear, and these are interests which, more than anything else, operate in contravention with the interests of other parties.

And so they feel a perfectly legitimate, natural jealousy toward their more successful, affluent rivals. In Moscow, Russian politics are stewing, and that's precisely why they regard "America" more warily than we do in the provinces, where nobody cares about the Moscow BS.

In Moscow they "do" politics; that's why they constantly strike various poses vis-à-vis America. They do business (forge careers, make fortunes) in Moscow, but they don't live simply for the sake of living. Because in order to live for the sake of living one needs to leave Moscow. They come to Moscow in order to do work.

Life isn't commutable in the provinces, it exists for its own sake, as it were—in all its hardship, its crudeness, its ephemeralness. In the capital there is too much money, the strain of centrality, an excess of everything.

The hoarding of surplus and its subsequent alienation are criminal in and of themselves; therefore, it is important to justify oneself, to find some internal excuses. By alienating that which doesn't rightfully belong to you,

you allude to precisely such a criminal, one who takes that which doesn't belong to him from the rest of the world. Hence, the figure of a rival appears: metropolitan anti-Americanism is a mirror image of the Muscovites' complexes, for they live at the expense of the rest of the country exactly the way America lives at the expense of the rest of the world.

What's more—America is always an event to us. Like something that isn't nearby. Like something that's impossible to see or touch with one's hands. For us to hear about America in the news requires that something happened there. It's been happening. In the provinces, on the other hand, life is entirely eventless; Great History is not made here, here they simply live. And that's precisely why America and the provinces pay no heed to each other—they exist in different dimensions.

There are, of course, Hollywood, Michael Jackson, and Coca-Cola, but all of these are part of a completely different history.

*Translated by Andrea Gregovich*

# You Are Not in Chicago, My Dear!

## Marina Boroditskaya

Dear friends and colleagues! I would like to begin with a warning. What you are going to read in the next ten minutes or so is totally and completely unscientific. It is not based upon any serious research; it is actually just a few notes by a lifelong interpreter and translator on some peculiarities of Russian and English manners of speaking: peculiarities that *might* but do not *have to* reflect certain ways of thinking or mental patterns.

Belinsky, a great literary critic of the nineteenth century, once called translators *the post-horses of enlightenment;* so you may think of this little essay as "Travel Notes of a Post-Pony."

I. Among the many interesting patterns that can be traced in Russian-English/ English-Russian translation, two tendencies have always struck me as both amusing and revealing. One is what happens to the English word *mind* in corresponding Russian phrases. The other is how positive English statements miraculously translate into Russian negative ones.

| ENGLISH | RUSSIAN (word for word) |
|---|---|
| peace of **mind** | peace of **soul** |
| presence of **mind** | presence of **spirit** |
| out of sight, out of **mind** | out of sight, out of **heart** |
| a sound **mind** in a sound body | a sound **spirit** in a sound body |
| a load on smb's **mind** | a stone on smb's **heart** |
| a load off smb's **mind** | a stone off smb's **soul** |
| What's on your **mind**? | What's on your **soul**? |

Shakespeare, from Hamlet's soliloquy:

| | |
|---|---|
| "Whether 'tis nobler in the **mind** to suffer" | "Whether 'tis nobler in the spirit to submit" (tr. by Lozinsky) |
| | "Whether 'tis nobler for the **soul** to suffer" (tr. by Pasternak) |

Shakespeare, Sonnet 116:

| | |
|---|---|
| "Let me not to the marriage of true **minds**" | ". . . to the marriage of two **hearts**" (tr. by Marshak) |

And, to crown it all:

| | |
|---|---|
| **mental** illness | illness of **soul** |
| **mental** patient | **soul** patient |

If you go on like this, you finally come to the conclusion that Russians have no mind to speak of and, consequently, have to do most of their thinking with either soul, or heart, or spirit. The political and economic results of this kind of thinking are too obvious.

Fyodor Tyutchev, one of the greatest poets of the nineteenth century, the golden age of Russian poetry, once wrote a few lines that later became his trademark or, as we say, visiting card (which to my mind is a pity, for he could have made himself a much better one). Anyway, here is his famous stanza translated by your humble servant:

> Perceive not Russia with a mind,
> Nor size it with a common measure:
> Its nature's of a special kind,
> Your faith in it will be your treasure.

To which a contemporary mocking-bird of a poet, by the name of Igor Guberman, wrote the following parody:

It's time, all bullshit left behind,
That Mother Russia got a mind.

But then again, on the other hand, if we proceed from the same set of *mind versus soul* phrases, it might lead us to a conclusion—purely unscientific, of course!—that English speakers tend to do at least part of their *feeling* with their *minds*. And, unscientific though it is, it can give us at least some notion of how America has finally arrived at the idea of *political correctness*. Obviously, it is rather difficult to do something about people feeling certain feelings or emotions that are not right to feel, if you try to do it with your heart or even worse, with this complicated and maybe nonexistent substance called soul or spirit. But if you use your mind on them, you can always think of something, like for instance changing or banning the words.

All this is closely connected with my next point, or linguistic tendency number two: English positive versus Russian negative.

Some of it, of course, must be blamed on grammar. Grammar is something you cannot change at will, because it just is. But then I've always had this utterly unscientific hunch that the grammar of one's native language leaves huge imprints on one's mentality. Or maybe vice versa; it is for psychologists to say.

Anyway, as you all very well know, English is quite thrifty with its negative forms. A single negative in a sentence is more than enough: "I have **no** relatives in Minnesota" or "I **don't** have cousins in Idaho."

While Russian thrives on double and triple negatives: "I **don't** have **no** relatives **neither** in Minnesota **nor** in Idaho" is a perfectly correct way of saying it in Russian.

Moreover, in some cases—the most tricky ones for interpreters and translators—an English **yes** actually needs to be translated with a Russian **no**. For example, the answer to "It doesn't often snow in Moscow, does it?"—"**Yes** it does"—in Russian absolutely has to be "**No** it does."

With the latter form one simply has no choice. But there are cases that cannot be blamed on grammar, when Russian speakers just freely choose the negative form of speech. Where an American customer asks the shop assistant: "Have you got this or that?"—a Russian would almost certainly say: "You haven't got this or that, have you?" I leave it to you to figure out the reason for this choice.

II. So, all the above-stated leads us to two different manners of speaking/ thinking that can very roughly be defined as rational plus positive and ir- rational plus negative. As interpreter at a number of international events, I have seen and heard both patterns displayed at their best and purest when- ever there was a challenge or some obstacle to overcome.

The English speakers' most common reaction is "What can we do about it?" Their way of dealing with a stumbling-block is removing it. After a little brainstorming they usually form a committee.

The Russian speakers' most common reaction is "What can we say about it?" (Which actually means: Why don't we all sit down and share our feelings?) Their method of dealing with a stumbling-block is finding a roundabout way. After long brainstorming they usually come up with something completely crazy but very creative.

Then all that's left to do is combine the results of the two brainstorm- ings and be happy.

As a native Russian speaker, I must also add that we function best under pressure. Which makes perfect sense, too: if you do most of your thinking with your guts (alias, spirit), plus you never see no way to change nothing, then all you can do is sing a beautiful song about it.

A classical example of this phenomenon is the world-famous Russian school of literary translation. It appeared and bloomed under Stalin's censor- ship when the best writers and poets "emigrated" into translation and chil- dren's literature. If Boris Pasternak, the poet and author of *Doctor Zhivago,* could publish his own work freely, we would never have got these wonder- ful translations of *Hamlet* and *King Lear* and *Macbeth* and *Othello* and what- not. If Samuel Marshak could write and publish whatever he fancied, maybe Shakespeare's sonnets and Robert Burns's ballads would not have become an indispensable part of Russian literature which they are now.

And maybe the most brilliant example of how this works is "Mister Twister," a children's poem by Samuel Marshak written at the beginning of the '30s. Marshak was pressured into writing a pamphlet bad-mouthing Americans for being racists. But he got creative and produced a really funny and charming and by no means hateful story about

> Mister Twister,
> Retired mi-neester,
> Businessman, banker,
> Billionaire . . .

which those of you who have been to Russia probably know. And by the way, it is Mister Twister who says to his daughter Susie: "You are not in Chicago, my dear!" when they cannot find a hotel for *whites only* in Leningrad and she suggests buying a house.

III. Just in case I have gotten too carried away—my next point is that things are changing fast. There is no more censorship in Russia, and both the school of translation and children's literature are quietly dying out. And America is busy teaching its Mr. Twisters a severe lesson in democracy without even bothering to make it funny and charming. As far as I know, quite a few children's writers and school librarians in the U.S. are complaining about the pressure of *political correctness* and the paranoid fear of *negative modeling*.

Take the following book, for instance: It's the Russian ABCs—a little verse for each letter of the alphabet—ordered by the Sesame Street International Project, written in Russia by your humble servant, censored and searched thoroughly for negative modeling in New York, argued and yelled about across the ocean, stripped of all bad words such as *scissors* (dangerous object?) and *toothache* (too scary for the kids to know?), and finally published in Moscow.

So I thought, maybe it's time indeed. Time for Mother Russia to get a mind, rephrase some of her questions to make them positive and learn to be creative without pressure. And maybe it's time for our American colleagues to learn to function under pressure and even censorship, to work their way around obstacles, to get out of their minds once in a while and think negative, which can be fun.

So maybe we could learn from each other and thus make it "a marriage of true minds." For we were meant for each other, weren't we? And yes, let us form a committee!

*Translated by the author*

# SPACES AND PLACES

## EVGENY BUNIMOVICH

American cities seem to be especially constructed so as to rid a Muscovite of his complexes. Before me, here, we do not even have a city, but actually a big village of sorts, with several skyscrapers comprising a business district, floating in a sea of varied yet quite identical houses with cropped green lawns. Here and there one glimpses the avant-gardist domes of a number of small churches, not to mention counting dozens of mosques and synagogues. The orientation is motley in the extreme: from superconservative to superliberal, whichever church you go to, whichever God you believe in is not that important—only that you have signed on to something.

The local population is bucolically guileless, smiley, simple-hearted, happy to greet any strangers they meet. The Russian village *banya* with a steamroom is successfully replaced by a five-minute walk near one's home, after which even at night one returns wet, red, sweaty, keenly feeling the pleasant coolness of the air-conditioner.

As everyone knows, there is nothing at all, alas, to look at in provincial America; geography takes the place of history. Of course, if by some fluke one finds a vestige of something on the order of Master Gambs's twelve-chair set,[1] Americans will treat it like a piece of the Coliseum wall and it will occupy an appropriately prominent place in a local museum.

However, despite what I have just said, please allow me to bring to your attention several subjectively chosen exhibits of possible travel destinations.

Exhibit 1. The Epstein Residence. It is not difficult to find Mikhail Epstein, the principal ideologue of our literature's *new wave,* in the Atlanta telephone book. There're more "Michael Epsteins" than you can imagine, but Mikhail—only one. His house, as you approach it in a thoroughbred

---

[1] A reference to the chairs in Ilf and Petrov's *Twelve Chairs.*

Toyota, is a midsize American affair, with a lawn, a terrace and sundry other American gewgaws and gimcracks. One step beyond the threshold and you find yourself surrounded by the ineffable Moscow kitchen bedlam, embraced by the man of the house and his countless progeny. Thus, the entrance to the Epstein lair presents itself as a tapestry, if you will, on Geppetto's wall. On which side lies the Field of Fools, on which is Wonderland? This you are free to decide for yourself.

Slavists, they know their business inside and out. You quote in their presence from the immortal poem *Moskva-Petushki:*[2] "In my opinion, the president's chair must be occupied by the kind of man whose crapulous mug one couldn't touch with a three-day beating. And are there any such among us?" You proceed to point out the classic text's striking actuality—and run right into their polite questions: Who is Venedikt Erofeev? What does it mean—*mug one couldn't touch with a three-day beating?* How can this be translated into English? And what has the President got to do with it?

And they're right—how *do* you translate all this into English? And what on earth has the President got to do with it, indeed?

Exhibit. 2. Margaret Mitchell's home. Besides Misha Epstein's abode, there is at least one other writer's home in point A. And what is Atlanta to the entire progressive humankind, after all, if not that momentous kiss between Clark Gable and Vivien Leigh? However, the home of *Gone With the Wind*'s author was nearly blown away right behind her characters.

In complete accordance with the inhumane laws of capitalism, they intended to remove the house and construct another building in its place. Passions that flared as a result around this proposed demolition mirrored the fuss surrounding Bulgakov's home on Bolshaya Sadovaya.[3] And the outcome was the same: thanks to the courageous efforts of several local *Bul-*

---

[2] By Venedikt Erofeev, tranlsated into English and published in the U.S. under the titles *Moscow to the End of the Line* and *Moscow Circles.*

[3] Meaning the building in which Woland, from *The Master and Margarita*, lived with his retinue during his stay in Moscow. The building was subsequently turned into a museum.

*gakovites* (Mitchellophiles?), the house was neither completely torn down nor restored to its former condition.

Thus it stands in the very center of this flourishing city like a decayed tooth. There is one hope: perhaps, in complete accordance with the inhumane laws of socialism, local officials, in order to celebrate some historic anniversary, will not only renovate it but will open a museum in it, too, to coincide with the occasion.

Exhibit 3. Office of the founder of the Coca-Cola Company. Readers, forgive me, his name is writ on water (I forgot it), even though his heroic deed is, in its own way, immortal. Yes, it was here, in Atlanta, that this empire was born, graphically demonstrating what the famed American entrepreneurial spirit can create from ordinary Russian *kvas*.[4]

As is the case with V. I. Lenin, in the city there is a Museum of Coca-Cola (for the public), and a memorial office suite in the company headquarters (not for the public, but by special invitation only). Since the recipe for this immortal carbonated drink is a closely guarded military secret, the museum basically consists of bottles from different countries, all looking different and all with the same contents, advertisements in all the languages of the world, and a countless number of flags from countries where one can find this beverage. In a way, it's like a WWII museum—it remains unknown, however, whether all these flags (our tricolor among them) were in a similar fashion tossed down on the ground in front of the Founder's Tomb.

The founder's office is austere and lofty, and does indeed remind one of our own founder's office in the Kremlin (the same epoch, the same deliberate *modesty of surroundings*). On the writing desk—several bronze plaques bearing inspirationally moralistic dictums executed in the founder's own handwriting: "Coca-Cola belongs to the people"; "Coca-Cola can only be created after one has stored in one's memory the knowledge of all the riches produced by humankind"[5] and suchlike (I'm quoting from memory). I asked

---

[4]  A non-alcoholic Russian beverage made from fermented black bread that bears a striking visual resemblance to Coca-Cola.

[5]  Paraphrasings of Lenin's dictums.

the guide: who cast these in bronze? The grateful succeeding generations? She replied: "He did. His own self. Thought them up, wrote them, brought them into being, placed them on the table—all by himself." Coca-Cola's *c*'s are always capitalized in Atlanta.

One acquaintance of mine, after having lived for a while in the house of a friend of hers who occupied a prominent position in the Coca-Cola Empire, complained about having become afflicted with persecution mania: a radio in the shape of a red can, an alarm clock bearing the company logo, the same logo on lamps, towels, pencil holders, bed linen, plates, napkins, and even on a cake of soap. The lady of the house herself wears cute little earrings in the shape of Coke bottle tops. The situation, in other words, straight from the old Soviet joke: a bedroom set for three persons called "Lenin's Always with Us."

Exhibit 4. Martin Luther King Memorial Complex. House. Museum. Gravesite. Also not without the spirit of the above-mentioned office in the Kremlin and the house in Shushenskoe.[6] But not just a raincoat or some random pair of shoes—MLK's socks. MLK's suspenders.

A powerful video loop. One of the demonstrations organized by Dr. King in the 1960s. Calmly, with dignity, a chain of peaceful black demonstrators marches. Each one holds a sign: "I Am a Man."

Nowadays everything is different, everyone is "politically correct," which some cynics, recalling the old Soviet days, suggest be translated into Russian as *ideologically uncontaminated.* Even in Dunwoody, one of the richest, absolutely white suburbs of Atlanta, the school director is a black man, and so is the chair of the literature department. A group of black children are specially brought in from the city on school buses—to study with the white children. Yet not one of the black or Latino colleagues I've met in the offices during the day appeared at parties in the homes of people I knew later in the evening. Ideological control, like a Bolshevik Party cell, is premised on people's behavior at work.

---

[6] The village Lenin was exiled to by Tsar Nicholas II.

And my home, as is well-known, is my fortress.

And now for something a bit different—in circumvention of American geography for the sake of a more complete picture.

The most important holiday in the large American city of Pittsburgh, Pennsylvania, is not Flag Day, Independence Day, or Constitution Day, as one might think, but the finals of the biggest river regatta in the state.

Everyone knows: something in the life of any provincial U.S. city has to be the biggest, the most important, or at least the first of its kind. *What* exactly is not all that important—a collection of Impressionist paintings, a hockey team, a waterfall or a university, a crocodile farm, or a river regatta.

The latter is what's being celebrated, then. In the center of the city, on a fairly small spit of land, the confluence of two rivers, somewhere around 300,000 people are amassed. Together with those gathered along the riverbanks, on the bridges and the shore—a good half the residents of this huge city. In the clearing they stood, sat, lay, ate, drank (no alcohol—otherwise, a swift and hefty fine), young and old, black and white, rich and poor, leftists and right-wingers, invalids in wheelchairs and metalheads in studs, babies in strollers and old ladies in shorts.

Then the fireworks began. Fireworks! They were not the steady, methodical, solid, pulsating bursts we're used to—or, say, the fanciful, well-calculated, elegant French flourishes. Far from it! To rhythmic music, in the batting of an eyelash, they just up and splattered the whole sky with the kind of blasts that combined everything at once—both our Russian might and the French refinement. Unstoppably, without a single pause, unsystematically and relentlessly, this went on for no less than half an hour.

And the spectators greeted with joyful roars the *mostest* of it all: the highest blast, the lowest, the loudest, the brightest, the most sparkling, the most golden . . .

I stood there in confusion like the surrounding protrusions of downtown skyscrapers. This was truly a powerful and grandiose, yet at the same time childishly senseless, chaotic display.

Still, to me the most grandiose and striking thing was not this orgy of super fireworks, but rather the very end of the festivities. Three hundred thousand residents of the glorious city of Pittsburgh simultaneously got up, left their places and went toward the entrance by a single tapering road, between two rows of stalls loaded with food.

I know, it may be difficult to imagine, much harder than picturing the grandiose fireworks—but in the enormous crowd not only was no one crushed, but no one pushed, or shouted, or even exchanged an unpleasant word. Small islands of safety formed around the children's strollers and invalids' wheelchairs. From time to time a flock of teenagers would squeeze through, and the way would open calmly. As soon as a congested area formed at the front (and this, of course, occurs every five minutes in a moving crowd), everyone stopped at once and waited patiently for the crowd to start moving again. And so those at the back did not crowd or push the people at the front. None of our horse-mounted militia, cordoned off areas, special passes for the privileged.

There were police around, to be sure, and when an officer came through the crowd on a bicycle, beeping a warning on his horn, everyone stood aside and let him through. Everywhere you could hear, "Excuse me"— which, as we know, in America takes the place of our Russian "blin" and "yo-moyo."[7]

They all went together—young and old, black and white, rich and poor, leftists and right-wingers, invalids in wheelchairs and metalheads in studs, babies in strollers and old ladies in shorts.

The American people.

Whom now, it seems, it is considered bad form to admire.

And I am not admiring.

I am just giving them credit.

And then we took an hour and a half to leave the fifth floor of a ten-story parking garage, but that's already another story.

*Translated by Dawn L. Hannaham*

---

[7] Mild Russian expletives, approximating, respectively "shoot" and "fudge."

# OTHERWORLDLY AMERICA

## OLEG DARK

When a Russian says "America," he has in mind the United States. "To go to America," "to live in America," and the like—it's understood where he'd go, or where he'd be. The designation "USA," "United States of America," is almost unused in everyday, popular conversation. It's only part of specialized discourse: political, journalistic . . . The name of the continent, even continents (South America, North), has become for a Russian the name of a *country.* It is as if the American continent and the United States of America were one and the same, or as if the States occupied the entire continent, even both continents, and there were no other countries in America.

Such an expansion, this hypertrophy of the United States, naturally places its privileged positions in a mythological context. Other countries, separate states on the American continents, "undoubtedly *are,*" as it were; nobody questions their existence. Canada and Mexico are only two countries, concrete geographic, political *places,* immovable. The United States doesn't so much expand in the Russian consciousness, as it may appear, as much as it floats, shifts, drifts. And along with it keep moving, drifting the U.S. denizen who were once Soviet citizens—Russian émigrés, or those permanently residing now in the U.S.: they haven't moved to America so much as merely continued moving, drifting.

Their position is *worrisome,* unstable. This is why departure to the United States has, for those seeing off the departees, been traditionally connected with greater anxiety and disturbance than departure to any European country, or even Australia. The fact that this drift of the United States typically becomes attached to the American continent, even limited to it (America!), can be explained by the general limitedness of the human mind's scope, its lack of courage: we do know, after all, that the United States is located in America. That is where it is found. But this knowledge (gleaned from textbooks) contradicts our *general sense* of the United States as a nomadic country. It can be said that for us the United States is everywhere and nowhere. We aren't quite confident in the fact that it actually exists. The unforeseen change of place by an object always erodes its existence, robs this existence of *solidity*.

Our uncertainty about the existence of the United States is not in the least contradicted by our frequent trips there, our occasional and temporary (i.e., one presupposing the possibility of return with *stories* to tell) being there. Every time one arrives in the United States it opens for one all over again. And it seems that however many times you arrive there (*to reside* there), you discover that place anew. This trenchant ritual of "discovering America" is quite different in nature from one's "opening" of Germany, say, or France. One cannot seriously speak about discovering either of the latter, in fact—nor of any other country, for that matter.

A first arrival to France or Germany (any place-name will do) revises preceding literary preconceptions of it. And on every subsequent visit these preconceptions, of course, are revised further, added to or subtracted from. All of this is only "new information," a correction or expansion of *prior knowledge*. And the more often one travels to one of the European countries (or any country besides the United States), the scarcer the new additional information, until finally one's knowledge of the country has become as complete as one can reasonably expect a foreigner's case to be.

But the "discovery of America" happens every single time; it is endless. "Travel through America" is a specialized literary genre, having a certain general significance: it is meaningful both for someone like Vassily Aksyonov[1] and an ordinary Russian citizen. Travel, by the very fact of its taking place, proves the existence of a country: it is impossible to travel through something which isn't there. Such a general significance does not exist in the case of one's travels in France or Germany. The significance of this "discovery of America" travel is just as considerable today as it was in the Columbus era: documented travel as a proof of America's existence, the fact that it *is*.

---

[1]  A famous Soviet writer, who has lived in the U.S. since 1981 and has written a novel about his travels there.

As a child, I knew one feeble-minded boy who used to claim that there was no such radio station as the Voice of America and that what we all listened to was deliberately broadcast by "us," our secret services, so that everyone would think it was from America. And the "jamming" (a popular term at that time) was merely for greater verisimilitude. What's interesting here is the senselessness of the assumption: why would "us" want to do such a thing? But the feeble-minded boy wasn't interested in this. The denial of the existence of the Voice of America is just one step away from the denial of the existence of America itself. "America" and its "voice" (imagine that this is not the name of a radio station, but rather the literal definition of a voice—which, of course, America ought to have, even though, wouldn't you know it, America as a country doesn't exist) was for him nothing but pure invention, falsification of reality, a bluff someone felt was needed for some reason.

The feeble-minded boy's belief reflects—albeit in an exaggerated, shameless form—the common *Russian stance.* (The feeble-minded have no shame.) The existence of America comforts us. Every nation needs to have an imaginary Promised Land, where it is good, where they will "receive us." And so the Russians say "our (*nashi*) Palestine" (possible variant: "*my* [moyi] Palestine"). In plural, of course "my" turns into "our." The possessive pronoun signifies property, a belonging, entitlement to, while the plural indicates a number of stops in infinite wanderings. In reality, of course, there is only one "Palestine," and it is inside you. But at every stop where you *land,* so to speak, *this land* becomes Palestine as well. America is the Russian Palestine. "My America" sounds very natural and harmonious in Russian. The expressions "my France" or "my England," however, strike one as even phonetically artificial.

At the same time, this "discovery of America" includes, as it did for Columbus, an element of error, delusion, falsification: we intended to open something else entirely. And, just like Columbus, we persist in our delusion. And when we do renounce it, our disappointment takes on an especially painful form. Such an acuity of feeling is never connected with one's disappointment in France, England, or Germany. For a Russian, the United

States of America forever remains a blessed, cornucopian India. And if it—the United States—refuses to play that role, it is here that the true acuity of feeling begins, eventually leading up to blatant (painful) animosity and hatred. This acuity of feeling in and of itself is evidence of disillusionment: it was preceded by the obstinacy of delusion. In setting out for America, we begin to *wander.*

In everyday Russian conversation the expression "to discover America" is persistent, omnipresent, even importunately so; it's as if this phenomenon itself, the discovery of America, would trouble us, torment our imagination. This commonplace metaphor signifies both the discovery of something well known, already discovered long ago—and something still capable of provoking surprise: "Well, you don't say! Discovered America, didn't you!" We ourselves laugh over this recurring surprise, but we can't avoid it. It is unavoidable. Interesting here is the phenomenon of the "well known" itself, which in every individual instance eventually becomes un-known, un-guessed-at. That which is well known erodes.

The ideal route to India, which stirred the imagination of every despot in Russian history, from Pavel I to Stalin, finds its prototype in the European tradition: the Argonauts' travel to Colchis in search of the Golden Fleece. Colchis or India—these are not simply specific countries, even if distant in time and place: each represents a *changed state of land,* just like there is a changed state of mind. This is land where the Fleece grows on a tree (just come and get it, pluck it from the branch—ah, but *how* do you get there?) and where the landscape is fairly bestrewn with treasures (all you have to do is bend down and pick up those rubies!). For a Russian such a *changed state of land* has always been the United States of America. The journey there is one for good fortune—the fortune of the Golden Fleece.

The journey for the Fleece is traditionally connected with the notion of a heroic feat: struggle for an exit visa in Soviet-Russian conditions, the saving up of money, some vague negotiations on the subject of a possible job placement. But the chief heroic feat is the very personal decision per se: to go, to leave, to part. Such problems with leaving don't arise in the case of one's departure to another country. The *changed state of land* is indeed connected with an attendant change in the state of one's mind. Hence, the heightened anxiety on the part of those seeing off the would-be Argonaut. The thing is, it is impossible to return "from America"—in one specific sense only: return the same person one used to be, unchanged. Departed as one man, then—returned as a different one. Therein lies the keen sense of American unreturnedness. You can go to Germany or France—and *nothing will happen to you.*

It is precisely this damage caused to one's mind *as a result of one's travels* which is embodied in the logic of the myth about the Argonauts. ("Damage" we will understand to mean—beyond any judgment on our part—every dent and bulge that was *inflicted* and which *was not there before.*) Jason sets out for the Fleece as a youthful, selfless hero, and returns as an ungrateful, treacherous and felonious man: both in his attitude toward Medea and in regard to his becoming an involuntary agent of her transgression. He returns a changed man. Or, in other words, *the old* Jason remained there forever, in Colchis.

But there is only one place *from which it is impossible to return:* the world beyond the grave. In the majority of instances dealt with in the mythological tradition it is literally impossible to return *from there* (they will leave you there), and sometimes it is impossible to return as one's former self—remember Hercules, Orpheus, Odysseus. For having seen, in violation of nature's dictum, the world beyond the grave and *returned,* they pay, like Jason for the attainment of Colchis, with the coin of further tragic fate or even agonizing death, enacted in similar fashion: both Hercules and Orpheus, albeit under different circumstances, were *torn up,* dismembered.

The world beyond the grave is that very *place of changed conditions:* from the deprivation of memory to the transformation of human reactions. And the world beyond the grave is a mobile place, too—its localization is not defined, it keeps shifting. "Utopia," as we know, literally means *without place.* Not only Colchis and India, but all the succeeding utopias, right up to modern fantasy, have been associated with the otherworldly also, and the journey there—with the agonizing surmounting of natural, elemental, *lawful* obstacles.

This otherworldly interpretation of America (the United States) is buttressed by its "overseas" location. The watery barrier of ocean is traditionally associated (and the association is almost forcible) with Charon's ferry. But let's keep in mind the fact that Canada or Australia are no less "overseas," yet neither gives rise to the Charon associations. In Russian classical literature there are at least two episodes in which departure to America is associated not only with death, but with suicide. This myth of otherworldly America has a long tradition.

In Chernyshevsky's novel *What Is to Be Done?* (1863), Lopukhov attempts suicide, but then it turns out that he went to New York instead, from where he later comes back under the given name "Beaumont." Here it is, a transformation registered in the *changing of name.* In *Crime and Punishment* (1866), Dostoyevsky most likely was responding to Chernyshevsky when he decided to realize a fictional suicide. Svidrigailov, preparing to shoot himself, several times calls this act "going to America." And with the kind of intonation which makes clear—where else would one go? For him, the impossibility of associating suicide with departure to any other place is self-evident. Finding himself by chance near a policeman before he shoots himself, he says: "if they'll ask, tell them that I departed, say, to America." It is doubtful that a Dostoyevsky contemporary would understand this "America" as anything different from the United States.

One would think that Dostoyevsky, in the context of this link between *death* and *departure,* could have come up with the name of any other country. Could have, yet . . . could not. This persistent, ineluctable connection between suicide and departure to the North-American United States is all the more telling here, considering that in the episode with Svidrigailov, Dostoyevsky was not *thinking* about America as such, he was writing of something else entirely. He used the myth of America only as construction material for his protagonist. This natural farewell "to America" took place in Svidrigailov's psyche—and prior to that, in Dostoyevsky's; thus, a spontaneous, subconscious (one needs not think about it being *on purpose*) departure to the U.S. is viewed here as a murder: of one's former self.

*Translated by Andrea Gregovich*

# DO NOT A GUN

## ARKADII DRAGOMOSCHENKO

For the traveler there inevitably comes a moment when his or her memories are converted into small change. This kind of money has the habit of disappearing with a clang as it settles darkly at the bottom of various fountains or in a variety of receptacles along passageways. Passageways are dimly lit, umbrellas sometimes lie in a pile "just in case." On occasion there's even a faint odor of basil in the air.

Memories settle at the bottom of words, turning what is seen in daylight into more-than-strange figures and into never-before-seen images. The dream spectator, the contemplator of the fleeting laws of impalpable universes, is easily recognizable on the streets—whether in Marseille, Petersburg, or New York. Their faces are lit by the flame of still unextinguished visions, their arms mechanically groping among shadows for something to lean on. Sitting on the stoop of a brownstone at Park Place in Brooklyn, I began to have the foretaste of a mysterious paragraph from an as-yet-unwritten letter to my friend Valery Savchuk:[1] "Like a millstone, the merging of space and dislocation of time grinds down previous experience—an experience that seemed unshakeable, had the self-assurance of allegory; it gave rise to a string of explanations that immediately freed time of all its obligations in arcades of metaphor which were bestowed in multitudes to the imagination." In truth all I was trying to do was remember the ineffably warm nights in the Old Port of Marseille.

I don't want to forget the plane trees—in spite of the fact that at present I'm finding it very difficult to apportion them among the cities. And perhaps it's not even necessary: at the back of the Community Bookstore on 7th Avenue, behind the books, I've happily discovered a small café.

Books, in any quantity, can be taken down from the shelves and brought into the café, to be read to your heart's content. They can even be taken out

---

[1] St. Petersburg writer and philologist.

into a small garden, where an ash tree out of Turgenev is wrapped around a plane tree. Without a care in the world and with a cup of coffee, you can now set to work as if in a library. Of course it's cooler out in the garden.

On one of the tables I find some pages left by someone. They contain a rather dry account of the history of the so-called Voynich manuscript—a manuscript of mysterious provenance, written in an indecipherable language or code that cryptologists of the time of its discovery were unable to break. In 1961 the manuscript was bought by the New York book dealer G. P. Krauss for twenty-four thousand dollars. Later its value was assessed at one hundred and sixty thousand dollars, but after a long and unsuccessful search for a buyer Krauss donated it to Yale University. The first known mention of the manuscript dates from 1666, from the hand of Johannes Marcus Marci, in a letter in which he explains that it was obtained by the Bohemian Prince Rudolf II for six hundred ducats, at the time an enormous sum.

Like the last time, the sight of New York, as one flies down into it, recalls nothing so much as a scullery of cockle shells at the bottom of an ancient galleon. The only difference is that it is submerged a bit higher, up in the clouds. As soon as you get used to hearing several languages spoken at once, the surroundings suddenly lose their fifth dimension and the world returns to the realm of normal things, such as the heel of my shoe, ground down from too much walking, the reflection of the setting sun cast with seeming indifference by a passing subway train on the Manhattan Bridge, the ring of a telephone, a receipt from a liquor store, or a tearful meeting with Avital Ronell in a labyrinth of offices at NYU.

As was the case five years ago, Chilean wine is readily available. Although Los Vascos is generally considered the best, I personally prefer the '98 Las Casas. Tower Records—that bottomless pit of music and whispers in which, in what now feels like an incredibly long ago spring, Sergei Kuryokhin[2] whiled away his sleepless hours—still stands at the corner of Broadway and Great Jones Street. NYU's School of Arts and Sciences has moved and is now located only a few steps from here. By the way, it takes six years of study to be

---

[2]  1954-96, famous Russian jazz musician and composer, founder of the group Pop-Mechanics.

certified to prepare Japanese sashimi. It's doubtful that they teach it at the university in spite of the fact that they call it a school of *arts,* and that on the floor below me I can see doctors in white coats. But the Japanese are tolerant. They even tolerate their status as a minority. In brief, they are able to deal with the "eternity" of the Big Apple without sacrificing the ability to express their obvious feeling of personal dignity. It's possible that this is not unique to the Japanese, and in part this is perhaps why I've never seen a single ad for chewing gum here, not even on television. It must be assumed that this is because no one chews it. But they do drink coffee! It's in fact fairly good and decently served. Starbucks, the nationwide chain of American cafés, is clearly not doing particularly well Downtown. A McDonald's-style café is still a McDonald's; but Italian cafés are everywhere in SoHo, and their prices are through the roof. One thing is certain: given the incredible pace of life here, there is no truth to our fairy-tale New York café with a single wobbly table and calico curtains. Nevertheless, one curtain did beckon to me from a pile of Chinese jade eggs and Soviet badges that were being sold at a local flee market: a faded reproduction of Edward Hopper's *Early Sunday Morning.*

The speed—or rather the slowness—with which the painting returned to its place in my head was discouraging, and it was only on Sunday, in New Jersey, that I saw something about which the artist kept silent. I saw the fine line that separates emptiness from plenitude. I recalled, like the memory of something that never happened and then sinks to the cunning bottom of words, to the bottom of the bottle, something that glimmers in Chekhov but that in Boris Akunin's[3] sequel to *The Seagull* pales with startling rapidity.

In New Jersey it's someone by the name of Fandorin[4] who seems to play the role of trivial ornament, something like that strip of Columbus Avenue with painted doorways and windows that don't always coincide exactly with the real ones. The prices here suit everyone's budget. This includes even Vladimir Kanevsky,[5] who has managed to dig himself a real sculptor's lair on the

---

[3] Akunin, whose real name is Grigory Chkhartishvili, is a popular Russian mystery writer.

[4] A stock character of many of Akunin's mystery novels.

[5] A contemporary Russian-American sculptor.

second floor. He bears this hell (ninety degrees Fahrenheit plus another 1000 degrees when he fires up his kiln) with the equanimity of a Roman legionnaire staring straight into an air-conditioner. Or vice versa. The important thing, he says, is that you can see the stars and there's a good bakery downstairs. He doesn't care when the electricity comes on or how the movers handle his sculptures that have literally just returned from a European show. And what's the use anyway when, in addition to everything else, "Indian summer" has descended? Everybody's on roller skates and nobody sleeps. It's a pity that Whitman never wrote any odes to garbage trucks. I think he could have started one off like this: "I celebrate and sing you, giant American garbage trucks / Devouring our past each morning / And with the ease of a serrated knife / Carrying off all traces of predawn dreams."

Happily, at the corner of Barrow and Mercer streets (I'm leaving now, have already left, it's Wednesday here), there's a piano bar called J. C. Winston's. On top of the piano there's a sign: Do not touch the piano, do not put a glass on the piano, and do not fire a gun. Inside, on the door, there's another: Respect Your Neighborhood.

This is probably just in case someone's got the keys of power in his or her pocket.

### Cast Me Some Soap

One of those unnoticed phenomena, or rather one of those phenomena that has imperceptibly become part of daily life thanks to the Internet and just as imperceptibly changed daily life itself, is electronic mail. However, those limp but tirelessly persistent lamentations by the defenders of the pen and admirers of Gutenberg—for some reason this reminds me of a recent summer conference, not of birds but of writers, in Moscow—about how we are precipitously abandoning our beloved galaxy, about how the good old days of the ruled page, neurasthenic rough drafts and postal horses are becoming part of the past, about how we are surrendering to the world of the visual image, have proven to be little more than a primitive framework to describe a rather different, independent course of things.

The picture that can occasionally be glimpsed in this design is a monotonous one, and full of a facile melancholy. On one side are the scribes, masters of an impeccable "rondo," equipped with candles, ink, night thoughts, and the date "Martober 2034";[6] in a word, everything that unhurriedly mourns for a kind of poetry that is disappearing before our eyes. On the other side a group of perfidious, virtual monsters wearing black leather gloves and helmets who take the stage armed with a terrifying jargon, whose lexicon is incomprehensible but whose clear intention is to destroy "what we cherish."

In reality, the logic of these changing textures and modes of writing bear witness to something altogether different and applies to their various manifestations. Generally speaking, each new mode seems richer than the preceding one; and while the new one does repress what came before it, it adds new possibilities to what already exists. Silent films were replaced by talkies. Then came color. And then a new format. Then nonstop television, from whose point of view the silent, black-and-white movies sometimes provide an unexpected bit of pure pleasure. However, the means by which new forms of writing subsequently influence "writers" is a history of a different kind.

In the course of the last ten or so years, with the creation of the Internet and the Web, we have seen not only a gradual revolution in the perception of time and space, and consequently of the possibilities of expression, but also—strange as it may seem—one other fundamental phenomenon: a return to writing, perhaps to virtual writing, but nevertheless to writing. It turns out that we have unconsciously come full circle, returning to "paper" in spite of all the ardent speeches in defense of the new, digital order of things. Indeed the Internet has turned us back toward the past because, as Adam Gopnik has written, the Internet is a kind of writing, given that it is literally *written* "from beginning to end."

It can of course be objected: even assuming that you are right, what is the "carrier" of *this writing* ('pis'mo')? Paper can be touched. A book is a tangible, physical object, moreover it has a smell: printers' ink, manufacturing chemicals, etc. And how priceless is writing paper itself, its special, unique odor and

---

[6] From Gogol's *Diary of a Madman*.

color, to which literature has paid so much homage! Finally, what separates the first, primordial sign etched in stone from the image on a computer screen? To this imaginary question I give the following answer: what is most important to consider are the changes in the concept of *materiality,* as well in the system of concepts—a process stretching back over the last one hundred years—relating to the very possibility of describing any material object whatsoever. This object, the description of which previously relied on the coordination of the concepts "beginning and end" (every object had both), is now conceived as some kind of oscillating point of a perpetual "now," a definitive account of which is extremely difficult, if not impossible, to obtain. Indeed, isn't it rather naïve to claim that we can feel a sign, as if it were a slab of painted, reinforced concrete that could be raised to the forty-fourth floor?

All in all, "to be online" signifies, on the one hand, a perpetual "now," real time, but on the other hand it means reading letters written by others; no less does "being on-line" also mean writing one's own words, which are addressed to another. Even game sites can't function without them. (Not to speak of pornography sites, with all their pock-marked explanations and doubtful stories of various kinds.) As for electronic mail itself, there is no way to deny its verbal character—of course, with the addition of instantaneous connection. But only connection, nothing more.

Even five years ago most of us relied on the telephone for contact, with perhaps a dozen or so letters written per year. This is not to say that there were no exceptions to this rule, champions of epistolary prose; but the aims of their passion were of a different order than ours. In their enterprise the border between personal journal and the outside world was, so to speak, effaced from the start, while the functions of interlocutor were transferred not to the "I" itself nor to an imaginary future reader but to a really existent recipient whose role was akin to that of a publisher.

Neither a telephone nor videophone offers the possibilities of e-mail, for this simple reason: *writing,* written language has the inherent ability to create a salutary barrier, a kind of second skin or distance that allows one to disappear from sight at any moment. This is a space in which no one can deprive you of the right to instantaneous solitude on this all too overcrowded, unlivable island.

NYU Professor Marek Skalsky has his office directly across the hall from mine. As far as I know he is the only person within a radius of fifty kilometers who, with unfeigned and malicious glee, beats on the keys of an altogether un-electric typewriter in what can only be called holy intoxication. It is certainly within the realm of possibility that the typewriter is some kind of mysterious part of his life project. This perhaps explains why so many of his colleagues, from various departments, sneak up to his door and, with an expression of mystical horror mixed perhaps with ecstasy, listen hypnotized to the banging of the keys, as if to a heavenly choir.

In order to connect with Professor Skalsky you've got to catch him in the hall or elevator. Knocking on his door is useless, for obvious reasons. His fax machine broke down sometime in the twentieth century. The sound of the telephone sends him into spasms of rage because the first words he always hears have something to do with questions about his e-mail address.

I drop in to see Eliot, a professor in the Slavic Department and a special-ist on Alexandra Marinina,[7] then return to my desk to write this last line: if I'm not right, then cast me some soap.

## In the Country

Considering the quiet of the morning and the placid expressions on the fac-es of the passers-by, you might take this world-famous neighborhood for a country village on a fine, cloudless morning. But this impression would be deceptive.

At eight-thirty in the morning the neighborhood is already aboil with activity, like hydrogen peroxide bubbling on a cut. Suddenly and irrevocably. The Dutch bought Manhattan from the Indians in 1626. At that time the is-land was covered with forests, and elk and moose rambled freely—in a word, nature successfully played its role of stern but beautiful mother until it was conquered by a tobacco plantation.

By eight you already have to elbow your way inside Café-Café on Green

---

[7] Popular author of contemporary Russian whodunits.

Street. The rustle of papers, a crepe de Chine crackling of notebook computers, cell phones trilling softly—a cup of iced coffee in hand. The ice gives
sharpness to outlines. I'm waiting here to meet with the documentary filmmaker Jackie Ochs, who has lived in SoHo her whole life. Recently the Museum of Modern Art has opened a Downtown location: Jackie's apartment
building shares its entryway with the new museum. "It's gotten safer and
cleaner." That's no surprise. Peter Aleshkovsky,[8] for example, was born in
the Tretiakovsky Gallery.

Both Jackie's apartment and the museum are located on lower Broadway, a few doors down from Houston Street. It's a stone's throw from my office to Green Street. In 1731 the English Naval Commander Sir Peter Warren
bought part of a plantation and, the chronicles tell us, built a marvelous estate
for himself. He called the area Greenwich. Jackie is supposed to have arranged
for a meeting with Betsy Sussler, the publisher of *Bomb* magazine.

In 1983 *Bomb* devoted several of its pages to materials about the culture
of St. Petersburg. In those days the magazine was still large format. The cover
photograph shows Boris Smelov[9] standing by a gloomy-looking Yekaterinin-
sky Canal. SoHo, in fact, is not technically part of Greenwich Village, which
ends at Canal Street: indeed the word "SoHo" simply means South of Houston. Everything north of it is "NoHo."

At the end of the nineteenth century the entire neighborhood was re-
built—indeed it was here that the practice of raising "poured concrete facades"
was first tried. Initially, its purpose was merely to reinforce the already-stand-
ing wood and brick structures in a mixture of "Greek Revival," "Palazzo" and
other styles. By the 1920s the population of the area radically changed: flout-
ing bourgeois values, the residents of Greenwich Village became famous for
their "free" lifestyle. In 1970 a powerful lobby of artists managed to have a
city law enacted that granted loft-space to anyone who could prove that he or
she was an artist. These lofts are protected by rent control, which means that
rents cannot be raised as long as the inhabitant continues to reside there. This

---

[8]  Moscow-based contemporary Russian writer.

[9]  1951-98, well-known Leningrad photographer.

literally compulsory attachment to SoHo was in part responsible for the difficulties encountered by the next generation of artists to find somewhere to live here—indeed in the 1980s they were forced to settle in the East Village. Such are the dynamics of this bit of micro-geography.

It's a five-minute walk to the offices of *Bomb*. Unfortunately, Betsy Sussler isn't there. We subsequently learn that she thought the meeting was to take place on another day. And that the person she was expecting to meet with was someone altogether different than me. Editors are the same everywhere.

"Timing. It's always a matter of timing," Jan Kroeze, who is Jackie's husband and head of JKLD Incorporated, says. "And time constantly changes direction."

Formerly a lighting director in various theaters, Jan turned to the world of *haute couture* in the late '80s and is currently one of its foremost figures. He tells me that lighting for the theater and for fashion are two totally different activities: "In the theater light is used to bring out a particular shade of meaning, to create the most appropriate context for the director's idea or to help in performance. In show business, in the fashion world, light is used either to make a woman look as attractive as possible or to create the desired style on the runway—romantic or urban, soft or harsh, and so on. But of course the most important thing is to make the woman look beautiful. Are the top models actually beautiful in real life? . . . well yes, how shall I put it? They're normal, nice-looking girls. After a weeklong fashion show we usually celebrate with a party . . . there's smoking, drinking, dancing, and the like. The girls look horrible, exhausted, totally worn out. That's when I go to work: I make the light soft, tender, delicate."

On the apartment's balcony Jan tells me about his incredibly tight schedule. Victoria's Secret has added a spring show for Cannes to run parallel to the film festival. This means he'll need ten fully-equipped trailers from Europe in addition to the three trailers of computer equipment that will be shipped from America; and it all has to be ready in a week. Generally the season starts in June—in Paris and Milan. In July they go to New York. Then September in New York again.

Jan tells me that his first payment for work as a lighting director was in the form of a suit. The suit cost twenty-eight thousand dollars.

"No," I hear Jackie say. "It's not worth waiting. Let's go to her place."

She means to Betsy Sussler's. But it turns out that Jackie herself can't go. I go alone. Everything's close by. One more iced coffee "to go." At her office they tell me that she's on her way to the office; or rather that she called from the subway to say that she was on her way.

The first issue of *Bomb* was published in 1981. The aim of the magazine was fairly simple: to allow artists to give their opinions about what they think about art, not only in New York but worldwide. Or more exactly: to create a forum for the discussion of the question of what makes art art. The main thing was to allow artists, critics, poets, writers, directors and musicians to speak directly to one other—the "interviewer" was taken out of the loop because the magazine's interest was in "the deeply personal" way that these questions were posed in the artist's own work.

By calling it *Bomb* the editors presumed that they would only produce a few issues—but the explosion lingered and the magazine still exists nineteen years later. In 1999 Gordon and Breach released three volumes of the best interviews: "Speak Art," "Speak Theater," "Speak Poetry and Prose." The press run of each issue is twenty-eight thousand and *Bomb* is read by approximately one hundred twenty thousand people. Advertisements and fairly serious material are published side by side. Imagining NLO with color advertisements for "Absolut" vodka and Italian shoes, I came to the conclusion that there would be nothing catastrophic about it. The photograph of a thing is quite capable of having no relationship to the thing itself. Just as an utterance about something concrete could be talking about something altogether different.

There was nowhere to smoke in this office. My iced coffee had melted but it didn't create more coffee. "Our editors," the title page proclaims, "include some of the leading figures of New York's art scene."

Can you guess when Betsy arrived?

## The Wheel of the House

It begins with a trailer: arrows flying, men on horseback, eagles soaring through azure skies, and all the rest, right out of Fenimore Cooper, then advertisements on subway walls and children's dreams. Gradually the narrative loses its way: there's a street, slanting snow, a low sky. When my luck changes we can name it: Petersburg.

Let's light the magic lantern, let's pass the hundredth video camera along our way, let's raise the blinds of a computer store in order to hear how softly the word "winchester"[10] can be pronounced and immediately take leave of advanced technology in order to open up the dictionary.

"Winch," the Merriam Webster dictionary tells us, is a "roller" or "reel," that is to say something that must be turned or wound—something that returns by its own power back to its starting point. In other words: an ordinary wheel, or from another angle: the wheel of fate (let's agree not to call it the dharma wheel). We should keep this in mind before adding the letters that make the word "Winchester."

Winchester has ten letters. Between the letters are gaps. From these gaps comes what we subsequently call meaning. At home, for example, these gaps sometimes take the form of raindrops unexpectedly coming through a window, of a barely discerned murmur heard through a wall at night, of a letter that describes a meeting with some melancholy-looking chess master in a pair of sunglasses long out of fashion, of the moans of lovers and stairwells.

Several stories fit into these nine, self-revelatory gaps. Their meaning is strange, in part mysterious. Each reduces some of the reliability of the other while simultaneously adding new dimensions that make it possible to overcome the one-dimensionality of conclusions and to imagine an occurrence (sluchai) as an intersection of a multiplicity of coordinates, which does not, however, deprive the accidental (sluchainost) of the attributes of divine irresponsibility.

The first of these stories (this order, without doubt, is arbitrary) is useful in that it allows itself to be told. It's the story of the building of a

---

[10] The word "winchester" in Russian designates the hard drive of a computer.

house. This story, which essentially coincides with a life, is nothing less than an epic tale, that is to say many intertwined stories forming a single, predestined channel in which the end of each takes us back to its origin. And in addition: back to our bewilderment.

One of them concerns New Haven, Connecticut, where in 1857 Oliver Fisher Winchester (henceforth to be called Winchester) quits a boring job in a men's shirt mill to set up a factory for the production of automatic rifles (in fact this kind of rifle appears to have been invented by someone named V. T. Henry but a "gap" is a gap and we can only guess why it is pronounced "in one way" and written another way). The rifle is patented and played no small role in the War between the States.

While time does its work of effacing the tracks gone with the wind and with the Winchester, we ourselves will take a peek at the confluence of these disparate episodes from a different point of view. From the point of view of Sarah Pardee. In my mind's eyes I see something akin to that well-known picture of Edna St. Vincent Millay: spring mist, a flowering apple tree.

In 1858, at age eighteen, Sarah Pardee married William Winchester, son of Oliver Winchester. A few years later, after the sudden deaths of her infant daughter and, soon afterwards, her husband, Sarah Pardee came to the conclusion that the souls of those killed by the Winchester (among their vast number were, by right, many American Indians) had not only taken her daughter and husband from her but were now coming straight for her.

It was in Boston, during a meeting with a female medium, that the illumination of imagination took more palpable form. There are no extant accounts of the details of their conversation. It can, however, be inferred that the medium not only confirmed Sarah Pardee's conjecture concerning the pitiless and indomitable nature of the spirits but also explained that there was a way out of the situation.

What form did this way out take for Sarah Pardee?

In order to avoid becoming the property of bloodthirsty and vengeful demons, she would have to (according to the recommendation of the clairvoyant) begin building a house, and this construction would have to go on eternally, ceasing neither day nor night; yet if these conditions (i.e., the never-ending construction) were fulfilled, Sarah Pardee's life would also surrender those boundaries so dear to human reason.

In passing, by the way, out of the corner of an eye, just like that, even some small detail—and suddenly it's totally clear how everything always and so smartly coincides! Sarah Pardee received a twenty million dollar inheritance and a tax-free, daily stipend of one thousand dollars. She moved from Connecticut to the Santa Clara Valley (it's not clear why: it was a wasteland, tumbleweeds everywhere) and bought an eight-room cottage which she immediately set to renovating. We will not describe how the "original" looked.

The "reconstruction" lasted until her death, which didn't occur until 1922. *Note:* Llanda Villa (once again, we don't know why the house was thus named), which comprises 160 rooms (some assert that before the 1906 earthquake there were 708 of them), is a work that has nothing in common with what is called "architecture," i.e., with anything approximating a "plan." This resistance to what the term architecture implies ("containing a high degree of system, structure or order") is a function of its very conception. Lacking its most important ingredient—*wholeness, completion, entirety*— Llanda Villa is, to an amazing degree, a project *contradictio in adjecto.*

This house-as-process, wavering like smoke in the imagination, became a never-ending epistle to spirits and demons, a missive abounding in intricate allegories, crafty displacements of meaning, ellipses. Together with that, the architectural strategy itself changed during the process of construction.

We do not know exactly when an important decision—whose meaning can be reduced to the following—was made: if there really are evil spirits, then there must also be friendly spirits. And thanks to this "doubling" or division, the construction was governed not only by the need to create an invisible or frightening labyrinth but also spaces in which friendly spirits could take shelter. It is not out of the realm of possibility that fatigue had done its work and that Sarah Pardee felt a consequent need for allies or even just some friendly counsel.

Perhaps this explains the house's lack of mirrors. It is no secret that the most complex and terrifying labyrinth of all is the mirror. Nevertheless, according to legend, the house has two mirrors, although finding them is almost impossible since they are so-called "roving mirrors." In the Orient it is believed that such mirrors appear during séances, revealing to the viewer a world of perfect symmetry. Let's agree that the word "almost" leaves room for hope. On the other hand, staircases ascending nowhere and then descending, or rising to the ceiling and ending there, doors (sometimes of a size that only a doll could fit through) giving onto walls, stairs with risers only two inches tall (the spirits must have gotten tired out on them), unexpected and irrelevant grillworks: these leave no hope of returning to the spot from which one left. The wheel of the house turns unceasingly.

For purposes of full disclosure we should add several other features: columns installed upside down, the number thirteen embedded everywhere—thirteen palm trees, thirteen windows in the indoor winter garden, thirteen openings in the drains of the bathtubs. As the poet John Ashbery writes: "The grandiosity of 'paper buildings' like Brueghel's tower of Babel, Boullée's funerary temples, Piranesi's prisons, or Sant'Elia's Futurist power stations have been realized, and by an amateur, a fanatically motivated little lady from New Haven whose dream palace was crafted with Yankee ingenuity."

I am not inclined to share Ashbery's opinion on this last point. At times it is neither sleep nor dreams that move us to actions that have seemingly no basis but which nevertheless gradually change the shape of the past and the time of the future.

It often happens in life that we experience something that fails to take intelligible form in consciousness, it disappears without a trace and our subsequent search for it can best be defined as an endless effort to recall some kind of tormentingly necessary but unreachable memory.

I believe that for Sarah Pardee the house was, in some sense, just such a path, an attempt to reach the memory of a memory, the secret of which was perhaps revealed to her only after death.

Nevertheless, I am still disturbed by one question: did Jorge Luis Borges know about Llanda Villa when he wrote his short story "The Immortal"? Yet even while asking this question I know that, whatever the answer, it changes nothing about the story of the wheel, the rifle, love and an endless letter to demonic spirits.

## At the Edge of the Maghreb

*The next night he did not know where he was, did not feel the cold. The wind blew along the ground into his mouth as he sang.*

—Paul Bowles, *The Delicate Prey*

*Not a Real Poet*

Does it matter to whom Gertrude Stein said that he wasn't a "real poet" and not an "authentic writer"? It is well known that she was more than willing to change her point of view depending on the conditions and requirements of "the laws of composition." In any case, what interests us here is not so much Gertrude Stein's literary passions as the fact that after this pronouncement and the "recommendation" that followed, the young composer—for in the 1920s Paul Bowles considered himself a composer—felt relieved: he owed no one anything and time opened up its gateway of dreams for him. Coincidences depend not so much on desire as on the density of existence.

Every voyage is a dream. We take as many of them as needed in order to build the circular maps of our movement backwards, to "our own beginning." One can only guess why and when Tangiers became for Paul Bowles that double point of arrival at the edge of the Maghreb, that point B, in which the role of *the other* was made his irrevocably but not without charge, and where two cultures, Europe's and Africa's, merged at the terrestrial rupture which is Gibralter.

It's something like a conventional hallucination, on whose boards the pleasure of intentional non-being is performed. This kind of hallucination is transparent, unemotional and similar to lilacs, which promise to reveal the secrets of transformation to those who are patient.

Bowles's readers can, if they wish, note that the qualities I've just briefly listed are also inherent in his work: his writing is fed on a disinclination to speak, his style more effaced than impoverished.

*Alcheringa*

In about 1973 Paul Bowles offered a kind of short essay in which he described his creative method or, more exactly, the geography of his style, a space of reading which clearly does not coincide with the scene on the page and that creates the impression of an endless approach to understanding which is simultaneously a withdrawal from it. One gets the feeling that something other than the reader's participation is called for. However, let us dare ask the following question as we gnaw our bewildered fingers and write into the corners of our eyes with perplexed needles: why is the novel *The Sheltering Sky* (which, by the way, made it onto the celebrated list of 100 Best English-Language Novels of the Twentieth Century) translated in Russian as combined effect of "desert, heat, flame, sand," plus the wandering English patients. And yet perhaps the death of our civilization is secreted in just these kinds of images.

Let us listen to Bowles himself: "Moroccan kif-smokers like to speak of 'two worlds,' the one ruled by inexorable natural laws, and the other, the kif world, in which each person perceives 'reality' according to the projections of his own essence, the state of consciousness in which the elements of the physical universe are automatically rearranged by cannabis to suit the requirements of the individual. These distorted variations in themselves generally are of scant interest to anyone but the subject at the time he is experiencing them. An intelligent smoker, nevertheless, can aid in directing the process of deformation in such a way that the results will have value to him in his daily life. If he has faith in the accuracy of his interpretations, he will accept them as decisive, and use them to determine a subsequent plan of action. Thus, for a dedicated smoker, the passage to the 'other' world is often a pilgrimage undertaken for the express purpose of oracular consultation."

Bowles writes of just such barely noticed passages—from one waking world to another waking world—in his short story "A Thousand Days for Mokhtar."

*Noise*

If for Maurice Blanchot noise emerges with the death of the last author (because the author is the final authority keeping silence in the world), then for Mokhtar this authority was his wife (his bride?), whose death causes the surrounding world to be filled with a noise of ever-growing and inexorable power. Mokhtar has a dream in which he kills a friend at the village market. Upon awakening he goes to the market and, in the middle of an unexpected argument over a debt that has supposedly not been repaid, Mokhtar realizes that he does not want the murder to take place. He says: "Last night I dreamed that I came here and killed this man, who is my friend. I do not want to kill him. I am not going to kill him. Look carefully. I am not hurting him."

Then the murder takes place. In the penultimate episode the judge addresses Mokhtar:

> "I have heard from the witnesses what happened in the market," said the Qadi impatiently, "and from those same witnesses I know you are an evil man. It is impossible for the mind of an upright man to bring forth an evil dream. Bouchta died as a result of your dream." And as Mokhar attempted to interrupt: "I know what you are going to say, but you are a fool, Mokhtar. You blame the wind, the night, your long solitude. Good. For a thousand days in our prison here you will not hear the wind, you will not know whether it is night or day, and you will never lack the companionship of your fellow prisoners."

Nothing special. It even provides the obligatory false signal—*in the silence of prison* Mokhtar remembers that he really did owe his friend the money and that the latter had a perfect right to reproach him for it. A perfectly literary short story. Narrated with complete clarity. But whether the story coincides with its meaning is another question. The things of the given world are unchangeable. They are what they are. At dawn a shard of rock-face appears to be the head of an old man, at dusk we notice that we are gazing upon the outline of a hand. The gradual change of color, of intensity, outline, of point of view, the vagaries of indigestion, some unintentionally received information, a book fallen on the floor—all this, and many other things, are "passages." Each object knows where the source of vision lies.

But in the space between the expected and what potentially exists outside of all perception and experience gleams a "third," the "coexistent condition" and its expression—"an expression," as Werner Heisenberg has written, "with an interim significance of meaning that cannot be expressed in everyday language."

Paul Bowles came into this world on December 30, 1910 in New York.

## *He Who Enters, Exits*

As a young man Bowles wrote a short story called "The Frozen Fields," about a young boy who dreams of having a friendship with a wolf who seizes his father by the throat and carries him off. It is hard to say whether this story is evidence of Bowles's tense relationship with his father or his acquaintance with the Pankeev's book on myths and legends. Certainly literature does not lack for fairy tales about wolves. There is no mention of the subject in any of his letters. However, in one, dated 18 September 1958 and written to a publisher eager for biographical information, Bowles does give a detailed description of the trajectory of his "passage." He explains that he was born in New York and grew up during Prohibition. Having completed secondary school at age 16, he enrolled at an art school. Quickly finding painting "silly," he transferred to the University of Virginia, "because Poe went there." After a semester he left Virginia and went to Paris, where he had already managed to get published in several literary magazines.

He got bored with Paris incredibly fast. He wandered around Europe for a time, then returned to America and the university, quit again, then went back to Paris. Apparently it was at this time that he met Gertrude Stein, was informed that he wasn't a "real" poet and that he'd be better off heading to Morocco.

Then came Algiers, the Sahara, the West Indies, South America,

Mexico (four years). In between he returned to New York and wrote scores for Broadway shows, "including among them the first William Saroyan play and the first Tennessee Williams play . . . Then I went down to the Sahara and wrote *The Sheltering Sky.*"

Sixteen years after his first visit to Morocco, he moved to Tangiers, where he established himself permanently. Together with his wife Jane. Their marriage has been the subject of numerous commentaries.

In the 1950s William Burroughs took refuge from his troubles there. His book *Interzone* tells a lot about the Tangier of that time. After Burroughs, it was Alan Ginsberg's turn to hang out there. Exactly who else came and went during those years is not known. In his diary John Hopkins mentions many names: Barbara Hutton, Brian Gusin, Princess Raspoli, Michael Forbes, Timothy Leary, Estelle Parsons, J. Paul Getty, Rudolf Nureyev, Yves Saint-Laurent . . .

*The Other Side of the Moon*

It wavers before me, this mirage, and I can't shake it; sometimes it's as though someone else's wearisome memory or premonition has taken insistent hold of me. I see the deck of a ship, I seem even to catch the scent of burning wood, of tar, salt and turquoise; and then I see *them,* seated in lawn chairs or standing by launches, frozen in the water's reflected light, holding their hats against the wind—in other words, the trans-Atlantic era. The dark sun of Okeanos shines down from all sides. Writing, I repeat (I must not lose sight of this), means dooming oneself to eternal tardiness in full knowledge that any story, even the most complicated one, even one filled with trembling, ecstasy and horror, will end in a tautology, with a metallic taste in one's mouth and a bitter burning in the eyes. The writer dreams of night while being sentenced to an omnipotent and eternal dawn, when even the banality of a shadow can't relieve the impersonal nothingness of the surroundings.

1984, Leningrad, Mechnikov Prospekt. To my complete surprise I've been sent two boxes of books by John Martin, the publisher of Black Sparrow Press. Among the tomes of Wyndam Lewis, John Wieners, Charles Olson, etc., there turns out to be two novels of Paul Bowles and a collection of his short stories. At present I don't have a single page of his work in my house. They all ended up at Vassily Kondratyev's,[11] although he told me that one of them, the collected stories, was given to Sergey Khrenov[12] for translation.

Slavoj Zizek has written that the horrifying impression made by underwater photographs of the *Titanic* is not a result of their symbolic over-determination, their metaphoric meaning—"it is not so much a representation as an inert presence." It is—he writes—the materialization of a horrifying, impossible *pleasure:* "We find ourselves in a forbidden zone, in a site that should have remained unseen: that which has become accessible to our sight is something like a petrified forest of pleasure."

## Tangerine Dream

Tangiers is one of the oldest cities in northwest Africa. Literature is one of the forms of public consciousness. Tangiers was originally inhabited by the Phoenicians. The hero of a literary work expresses what is most typical of his time. The Carthagenians drove out the Phoenicians, and the city was later taken by Rome. Russia is a kind of hallucination. There is no such thing as a "passage." The term *thanatos* does not appear in the works of Freud; however, according to his biographer Jones, Freud did make use of the word in speech. The Arabs took Tangiers in 705, but did not make it part of the Ottoman Empire. Portugal ruled it in 1471; in 1923 it was made part of the international zone. The river Mao has its source in Tangiers, then turns east and empties into Lake In. There are many horses of a kind called *bo.* They have a white coat, a single horn, and a tail like an ox. Their whinny sounds like a human scream. When mandarin oranges began to be sold in Tangiers, their name was changed to tangerine. Surely

---

[11] 1967-99, St. Petersburg poet and translator.

[12] This seemingly simple genealogy in fact bears an important and disturbing subtext. Both Khrenov and Kondratyev, relatively young men, died before they could finish their translations of Bowles: Khrenov fell out a window, Kondratyev, off a roof. Their friend Alexander Skidan was the one to finish the Bowles translation.

some of us still remember the band Tangerine Dream. On December 10, 1999, in the Italian Hospital in Tangiers, which is located close to the site in which the film *Casablanca* takes place, Paul Bowles died.

## Weekdays

Professor V. Savchuk
9/21/00
19:17:03

Dear V. V. S.,

I'm on the ninth floor, which as you know is a lucky number and was of service to the beautiful Beatrice.

I live on Washington Place, which is actually a tiny alley, a kind of park in the middle of Manhattan, between Washington Square and Broadway itself. The building seems to be a pre-war construction, probably from the 1930s, fifteen stories high and permeated from top to bottom with the glass canals of pneumatic mail tubes: just to look at them, even in passing, immediately transports the soul to that strange era of literary scandals, publishers' *soirées,* and trans-Atlantic cruises. The transom of my apartment window—the window covers the entire wall—is made of several strips of thinly plaited cast iron. By the quality of sound this street suggests a Stradivarius—even the most indistinctly murmured word, uttered somewhere down below, echoes and re-echoes throughout the room. Polyphony, it would seem, is inherent not only to poetry.

The immediate area around the building is considered part of the campus. Indeed the local police are not called by the usual term, *security,* but rather *protection.* You'll have to agree, that although small, there is a difference of semantics.

It's a forty-second walk from my apartment to work. In the rain I don't even have time to open an umbrella. My office gives directly below onto Broadway. The traffic light on the corner has been decorated by a local artist with bits of broken coffee cups. Very colorful, and it'll be there until the Second Coming. The classes I teach take place in two different build-ings: in Tish Hall, a vast, although not especially tall, terra cotta struc-ture (fifteen stories not counting three underground floors), and in the main building of the School of Arts and Sciences. Sixth Avenue is totally mysterious. It heads north and then abruptly ends in the sky, at Central Park. It's quite possible that it was originally designed as an exit route for all the world's tribes. Its capacity would certainly allow for it.

The Slavic department, which is located on the sixth floor, contains not only professors' offices but a small departmental library and administrative office, with a computer, printer, lamp, chairs and shelves, telephone, coffee machine, and the like. There is also a series of "conference rooms" in which the classes themselves are held: the rooms are large (thirty to forty square me-ters), with sound-proofed walls, impressive oval tables and straight-backed chairs (all of wood), and enormous leather couches lining the walls that must be avoided at all cost because if you fall into one of their beckoning arms all hope of surfacing on the waves of being must be abandoned.

Three minutes away, around the corner of the hall, is Avital Ronell's office. Her door is always open. She herself is seated in front of her Mac and wearing a Chinese straw hat. The kind the coolies wore during the construction of the great California railroad. She has the habit of wav-ing a friendly hand to passers-by. By the way, one of my first days here, while I was wandering around looking for a water fountain, who should I run into but Professor Derrida (he was looking for the exit)—but he disappeared and I haven't seen him since. Nevertheless strange things continue to happen periodically—this morning for example, walking past an office, I noticed, on the list of people signed up to meet with their faculty advisor, the name Walter Benjamin. It's hard to say with whom and about what he was intending to speak . . .

It's possible that I'll meet him at a party—these faculty parties that are a natural disaster, since they're inevitably held during the work week. Usu-ally they are scheduled during the first month of the semester so that we can "help to get to know each other better." Wine, cheese, and mineral water are served. That's all the provisions we get for this kind of bivouac. Last time a professor in a neighboring office brought a bottle of home brew—everyone greeted the sight of it with enthusiastic exclamations, but they were afraid to drink it.

But let's head home. Within five minutes walk in any direction are numerous bookstores. Feeling an irresistible need to give my eyes and brain a brief workout, I stop at a few of them on the way: how can a mind unprepared for such a quantity of books and titles stands up to the experience? I don't know where America ranks in the list of "biggest country of readers in the world," but it seems that here even the homeless, whose numbers appear to be declining catastrophically (the grim reaper? emigration to Russia? submerged to ocean depths by submarine? or just turned back into phantoms?), cart around a couple of piles of books. For two days running I've noticed one homeless fellow, on the steps of the Arts and Sciences building, with a book on the art of Mauritanian Spain. And you won't believe whom I saw a few days ago at the Grove Street Path Station: Marat Gelman.[13] He was heading up to Rockefeller Center. Reading the instruction manual for his new mobile phone.

But that's not the subject I want to talk about, not reading, to which I've once more got to get used to; it's about the incredible semiotic saturation of the city that I want to speak. It would be perfectly reasonable to conceive of New York as a gigantic letter, the backside of which is turned directly toward us. To a certain extent, this is what accounts for the city's extraordinarily high level of mental and emotional saturation, making it one of a kind.

What didn't we talk about, Misha Iampolsky[14] and I, as we wandered unhurriedly among book stalls and bookstores between Bleeker and Mercer streets! Our conversation was like our walk itself, branching off whimsically, flitting from one subject to another, before finally focusing on the history of the relationship of Diderot and Falconnet, to their fifteen-year correspondence on the subject of the eternal and the ephemeral, during which Diderot

---

[13] A leading contemporary Russian art gallery owner, publisher, and political activist.

[14] Mikhail Iampolsky, a contemporary Russian American philosopher, literary critic, and NYU professor.

unexpectedly dropped a line about art's ability to express adequately an inner state—and it ended with these Italian words: *esse Pulcinella!*

According to Iampolsky, this phrase has to do with a once well-known story about a Venetian monk. This monk, enraged by a delirious crowd that was surrounding a street Pullcinella, screamed out: "You're looking at a false Pullcinella, a pretender! The *real* Pullcinella is over there!" And he pointed toward the crucifixion.

Perhaps the monk's name was Savonarola, perhaps it was something else. History is silent on this score. As we weren't in position to resolve it, we instead took a seat at an outdoor Italian café. It was sunny and windy. I ordered espresso, Misha ordered tea.

Each day my walk gets longer, simplifying the landscape. By the way, every morning, at Union Square, which is about ten blocks north of here, the local peasants sell agricultural products. The corn is splendid, you boil it for three minutes and it's incredibly tasty—with blue cheese and wine, of course.

Soon it will be time for me to make another pilgrimage along the shelves of Chilean wine. It will probably include the Italian and French shelves as well. There are even some very fine Spanish vintages to run across. Vino Tondonia Reserva 1993 for example, or even the august Marquess de Cacares Rioja.

All for now.

Forever yours,

ATD

October 2000
New York

*Translated by Thomas Epstein*

# Nine-and-a-Half Americas

## Max Frai

1. My first America is an imaginary one. It does not exist at all, and never did. As a child, it seemed that grown-ups had invented America. But what for? They knew what they were doing. They had invented bogeymen to keep children from climbing into the attic. They had invented Young Pioneer heroes who died horribly to coerce children into following the rules and studying hard. They had even invented vitamins to force children into eating tasteless, slimy boiled onions, spectral petals that swim mindlessly in every bowl of soup. So they had invented America in order to inspire fear. As I grew older, the formula became more precise: they had invented it for propaganda. To keep the Soviet people from relaxing in the absence of an external enemy. But I was happily oblivious to words like these as a child.

And then from time to time we saw pictures of American life on television—the way you can see aliens from outer space in the movies—they seemed pretty much the same thing to me then. But Vovka down the block said that there were no aliens in outer space, just our own cosmonauts. Vovka was big, in the sixth grade, he probably knows what he's talking about.

Still later, I was childishly confident that America had been invented by mean-spirited grown-ups as the setting for innumerable jokes and shaggy-dog stories that were wildly popular in my circle of acquaintances and friends. They provided various funny explanations: where American things came from, and where people really go when they say they've gone to America on business or as tourists: whether they've been hypnotized into thinking they've been on a marvelous journey, or simply cowed by blackmail or violence into corroborating the existence of an imagined country beyond the ocean. We enjoyed ourselves immensely. But in February 1994, when a rented microbus conducted us from Kennedy Airport, and the black silhouettes of the Manhattan skyline reared up ahead against the fiery background and lily-white smudge of an early winter dawn, my heart nearly stopped in terror. We were about to penetrate into the two-dimensional space of a glossy postcard, to pass into an imagined, illusory reality. The obvious question then, and even now I sometimes ask myself, was where the hell were we?

2. My second America is related to the first, in the sense that it really was imaginary. This America derives from popular movies, the basis of a beautiful life in all its manifestations: from the heroic confrontations of cowboys and Indians to Audrey Hepburn, who has to have breakfast at Tiffany's, of course, and supper who knows where. The America of Coppola and Tarantino, of gangsters and cops, of clandestine parties of bootleggers and the happy, orange-headed pumpkiny horror of Halloween. Philip Marlow shoots back at scoundrels without letting go his glass of straight whiskey, Jack London's Smoke and Shorty swim on golden sand, Mickey Mouse wolfs down a hamburger with a cold Coca-Cola, and Marilyn Monroe sings like a nightingale, twirling her appetizing backside to the joy of all the other human children.

Beyond our wildest dreams, ah.

3. My third America might as well be the Land of the Dead, the place where my acquaintances and friends, in their own good time, went off to forever. To the West, to the sunset, to the dying sun, in full correspondence with ancient myths. In earlier times it was reckoned that from there, from America, there was no return. As for those of us who stayed behind, we never expected to go there. Therefore we said goodbye forever, saw living people off as if they had died, kissed their brows, and froze to the spot with grief.

Fortunately, this version of my America has long since grown old.

4. And there it is, my fourth America, the America of literature, the patrimony of the people of the Word, which, as we all know, precedes the act (and I am not fully certain that there ever has been a succeeding act). No need to list my favorite writers: the list is too long, a good hundred names well known to the world. I'll just note that a book by Thornton Wilder, *The Eighth Day,* fell into my hands in a library in the Ural village Tavatui

during the winter of 1984 and, if it didn't exactly save my life, it certainly saved my mind.

In particular, the structure of this very essay, the account of nine-and-a-half Americas instead of a single integral picture, is in its own way a tribute to the memory of the celebrated Theophilus North, who explained to me, along with everything else, that each city is Nine Cities, "some superimposed, some having very little relation with the others—variously beautiful, impressive, absurd, commonplace . . ."

5. I'd consider my fourth America the crown of creation if not for the fifth—the America of mysteries and miracles.

It's clear that my fourth and fifth Americas are not simply woven together, but bound up into several sailors' knots—it's impossible to unravel them. And there's nothing to unravel.

The map of my fifth America is a map of deserts, forests and putrid swamps, dappled with ancient Indian curses, tattered by the thorns of hallucinatory cacti and fouled with the excrement of rabid lizards. In the skies of my fifth America kites are swooping, and down on its earth unwashed shamans walk, and the sound track to this idyll is provided, of course, by Jim Morrison, who else?

6. And so we get to Jim Morrison. My sixth America, if not the motherland of current art, is still The Promised Land. Andy Warhol's Factory works nonstop, the boss has locked himself up in his bedroom with his "wife-tape-recorder," he treats himself to chocolate-covered cherries, for three hours he flutters around the telephone with his best girlfriend. Other things, people and events revolve around this eternal child like planets around the sun. This is an extremely harmonious and self-sustaining world. I like it very much.

7. The seventh America is deeply repulsive to me. This is the America of informers, hypocrites, bureaucrats and lawyers. The America of legal wrangling and civil suits, in the course of which irresponsible idiots are awarded

huge amounts of money from companies that don't provide special, useful instructions about their products for irresponsible idiots. An America of spurious, deceitfully interpreted political correctness, offensive to all participants in the process of human society. This is the America where passersby will not even think of offering help to a person who is dying in the street, because they are afraid of being sued. I won't go on: it's boring and obnoxious to go through it all.

8. The eighth America is one I happen to have visited. Strictly speaking, this is not even America, but a single city, New York.

I flew into New York with a friend in February of 1994 and stayed there until about March 10th. We had an exhibition at the Ronald Feldman Fine Arts gallery; we thought this was really, really terrific. We lived in a vast loft on Green Street in SoHo; the resident parrot took care of us, and we fed it in return. The elevator opened right into the apartment, and this detail drove us crazy, made us feel like heroes of a fantasy film, more utopian than anti-. . .

Every morning we went to the gallery on Mercer Street and set up this damned exhibit. We labored for twelve hours running, returned home, ordered take-out from a Chinese restaurant, then wandered around SoHo, stopped by bars, tried unfamiliar cocktails, listened to unfamiliar music, looked at unfamiliar faces, tried to get our fill of a completely different, incomprehensible, but entrancing life: just in case.

Bar 88, which took its name from the number of keys on a piano and is located somewhere in Greenwich Village, is the only one whose name I will never forget. I'll definitely look for the entrance again when I get the chance, but have to confess it will be more by instinct than by memory.

A pianist played there in the evenings, most of the clientele were of indeterminate sex, a lady with the appearance of a professor took my coat in the coatroom—in the deepest part of my understanding I knew this had to be the ideal bar!

A lady dressed in a dark leather man's suit behind the bar sang stupendous blues, successfully mixing cocktails and dumping cigarette stubs out of identical white ashtrays at the same time. I especially liked the cocktail she made called The Breeze: how many gallons of that liquid—pale pink, deceitfully sweetish, but in essence fiery enough to blow my head off—did I consume during those amazing evenings—God only knows.

The Feldmans—Frayda and Ronald—treated us gently, as if we were country cousins. They filled our pockets with money and good advice, took us to eat in an Italian restaurant, urged us to drink only decaffeinated coffee (advice we hardly ever follow, better to cut out coffee completely). Ron entertained us with stories about his own childhood; Frayda tactfully took care of all the details. Her colleague in the gallery, marvelous Peggy Kaplan, invited us to visit and for several hours nonstop photographed us for some album of hers. We have never been so inhumanly handsome as we were in Peggy's photographs, and, it must be understood, we hardly expect to be again. Chuck, the chief installer at the gallery, waved an English-Russian phrasebook in front of our noses and painstakingly pronounced his favorite sentence: "I have a back *ack*." He did not bother to learn any other Russian sentence. Obviously, he had decided that you couldn't ask anything of someone with a "back *ack*."

In New York we were very young (you always become a few years younger in a foreign country than you are at home, a strange effect) and, apparently, inexcusably happy. So passersby smiled at us, sidewalk vendors waved at us and threw us compliments. This became clear, by the way, only much later: it took us at least a week to understand the English you hear on the streets of New York.

And I still keep in my closet a pair of dark glasses with multicolored frames, which I bought for eight dollars from one of the involuntary witnesses of that happiness. It's impossible for me to wear them anymore, but my hand refuses to throw them out, although I usually discard old things with pleasure.

9. The ninth America is that one through which I will travel someday. I want to cross it in a rented car, from the northwest to the southeast, and then, along the other diagonal, from northeast to southwest. I usually en-

joy the roads I ride on—I see no reason why American roads should not be a real pleasure for me.

It would be good to go everywhere in America, look into every God-forsaken corner, flirt with the winds, get lost on the streets of a big city—let's say, L.A.—and then discover myself in a highway motel, somewhere on the far side of this imaginary land. To fall asleep in a field, sprout like the dejected grass, wake up in the morning and, as if nothing had ever happened, keep going farther on. To eat tasteless cherry pie in a roadside diner, close my eyes, swallow bitter ocean water, come to the surface again and lie for a long time on the sand, wiggle my fingers and my toes: I'm alive!

One day all this, of course, will happen to me. Sooner or later, one way or another, it will happen, for sure.

I know.


9 1/2. And then there is America in the subjunctive mood, that America which never was and never will be real for me. The America where I might have been born into an American family, lived an American life, eaten American food, drunk American drinks, slept with American boys and girls, raised new American children and with difficulty imagined that some people get born in foreign countries.

*Translated by J. Kates*

# GONE WITH THE WORLD

## MARIA GALINA

Alas, our impression of America (politically correct, handgun in holster) is formed primarily from films. There are so many deserted factories and automobile cemeteries where the enemies of everything that is good abuse and torment the average, ordinary American. And the average, ordinary American lives in a good house, has a good wife and a good job; he makes his career, his money, and his children; he's a very law-abiding and peaceful man, but if danger begins to threaten his career, his money, and his children (they usually kill the wife off right away), he takes up his handgun and runs out to defend traditional American values. And then he runs out to his psychoanalyst, and then he calls his lawyer right there in the office. To escape the people who are chasing him (and they almost always chase him), he travels in a very dirty underground train or a very chic car, hitting the gas from time to time and swerving from the passing lane onto the sidewalk. He also has this weird characteristic of getting drunk from a single tumbler in a half-lit bar. That's about it. Woody Allen doesn't count. He's practically one of *us*. We understand him. And that's frightening.

Generally, resemblances alarm us more than differences. If everything there is like everything here, why the hell are we dreaming of getting there? Why dream of Brighton Beach, Harvard, Florida? An altogether different image of America has been preserved to this time, somewhere in the mysterious recesses of the soul—an image of the promised land where one could still go during one's lifetime. And then everything would be good.

Our ex-patriots, now naturalized, come here to satisfy their nostalgia, and we want to touch them, pinch them—could they be real? People are careful with them, like with demigods or the terminally ill. I should say so! After all, they have returned from the place of *no return!*

Plus they behave—honest to God—strangely. They ask about incomprehensible things, demand fresh-squeezed juices and purified water. They complain of diarrhea. The majority of them are Slavists, for some reason. Especially among the second generation.

They love us for our nightmare—they professionally analyze Varlam Shalamov's short stories and the film *Khrustalyov, My Car!*.[1] They utter easily the difficult word "Solzhenitsyn." We feed their fear. They feed our dream of a paradise on Earth.

It's a mutually beneficial exchange.

And the one-hundred-percent American, borne on God-knows-what wind to Russia, we watch like we watch the mentally ill. This person is permitted things that are not allowed to our people. Talking nonsense. Getting into stupid situations. Farting and belching—and then, looking impertinently into our eyes, saying *oops*. Discussing the difficulties of his or her intimate life. It's generally easier to get into intimate revelations in a foreign language—there isn't that emotional heat. It's not really "language" (there's only one of those!) but a method of communication—you say only what you want to convey in words to your partner in conversation. A foreign language exists for that very purpose. For saying what you can't say, no way, no how, in your own language.

The September 11 shock was too much like the movies! We've seen it so many times . . . Replay, another replay . . . Slow motion . . . Another showing in the evening. Too beautiful to be the truth, too cinematic. And the sheer scope of these Americans! Everyone immediately found acquaintances who had worked on this or that very floor. For some reason it turned out that this very person on this very day had been late for work. Pure, ineradicable Russian sloppiness. A legend. One went crazy, tormented by not feeling guilty enough, and is to this day seeing a psychoanalyst. When he gets out of bed after drinking heavily.

The most incomprehensible part, the most irritating, is that in no way can the perception of America and Americans be reconciled with the perception of American literature. Anyone in the Soviet system with any higher

---

[1]  A film by Alexei German.

education treats American literature with more than awe. Salinger is for us a cult writer, Faulkner is good, Melville is a genius. Hemingway is our everything. Young people today wouldn't remember—although I do—that in every decent ETW apartment (ETW: engineers and technical workers, the foundation, the bread and butter of our culture) there always hung two portraits on the walls: Yesenin with a pipe and Hemingway. It seems like he had a pipe too. And there was American science fiction, which the average Soviet person possibly knew better than the average American—Ray Bradbury and Clifford Simak, Isaac Asimov and Robert Sheckley, Kurt Vonnegut and Harry Harrison. At one time, long ago, quoting those writers served as a kind of watchword, the code of an entire generation. And then there were Richard Bach and Ken Kesey . . . Phillip K. Dick . . . Frank Herbert . . . Ursula Le Guin . . . Carlos Castaneda, finally . . .

And we all got over them. Over American writers. We got over them, patted each other sternly on the shoulders, produced our own young prose, sent a few of our scriveners to America—just to show them, to even things up. Let them sit there in their Harvards, let them teach American housewives how to write real Literature. They blew over the Atlantic as the distant apparition of a distant nation. They howled wildly—"Whoooooo!"—and then they were gone with the wind.

*Translated by Jennifer Croft*

# AMERICA OF THE MIND

## SERGEY GANDLEVSKY

*The border held mystery for me . . .*

—Alexander Pushkin

"You young people only have America on your mind," my elderly relative
used to say, letting me know that there was no sense in wasting his breath
on a nursling like me. The conversation easily could have moved, by the
way, into the advantages of a multiparty system or the true author of *Quiet Flows the Don*—it didn't change the issue: nothing but America on my
mind, and that's the end of it. My relative was not a typical caricature of a
Soviet pensioner. Not at all. But from the altitude of his age he counted all
who appeared in the world noticeably after him as part of the same tribe of
"youth." (These days I commit the exact same sin.)

Most likely, he didn't mean us, but the previous generation—the Stilyagi of the Sixties.[1] In contrast to the model images of that highly gifted
generation, we didn't "make life" from America, hearkening to jazz under
the photograph of Hemingway and calling each other "old man." We devoted all our free time (and it was all free) to Scythian drunkenness, which
inevitability presupposed seditious speech—as though, in fact, verbal sedi-
tion itself was sold under the guise of foul vodka, otherwise known as "Volga
Dawns," or cheap port wine in half-liter bottles with dirty lopsided labels.
And it was precisely in the collective drunken profession of our Neanderthal
anticommunism that the United States of America came in very handy.

America, vis-à-vis the USSR, represented a kind of anti-country, a
state in reverse, and we, malcontents and insolents, cracked jokes list-
lessly, wandering around Moscow half-drunk and changing the capital's

---

[1]  The "Stilyagi," or "style hunters," began appearing in Moscow by 1949, adopting an American sensibility that included zoot suits, chewing gum, greased hair, and jazz.

familiar toponimics 180 degrees, "trans-Atlantic" style—the Regress Theater, War Boulevard, the Anti-Soviet Hotel.[2]

(Subconsciously, probably many of our fellow countrymen did indeed hope that the world's laws—including the trans-Atlantic and material ones—were not written for the New World at all, and tend to diminish, as it were, with the rotation of the globe counterclockwise, almost petering out in America, that ultimate manifestation of the West. How else to explain the childish carelessness with which the gray-haired, more or less respectable and prudent people at the end of the 1980s, when "The West" kicked open the door of the Country of Soviets, hastened to lend money for a fantastic percent to fly-by-night banks and even to the first Tom-Dick-or-Harry, as if none of us was ever taught in high school the laws of conservation of matter and energy? Personally well-versed in these laws, Yury Karabchievsky,[3] an engineer by trade, once troubled the delight of some neophyte investors from among the ranks of yesterday's destitute bohemians: "Things must be pretty bad in the economy if money is coming to punks like us." He really saw into the crystal ball. Now, it turns out that in some deep sense, my surly relative was in part right about the "America of the mind.")

All through the Eighties we counted on Uncle Sam the way we had, as little children, on Uncle Styopa the Militiaman, the Soviet version of "Officer Friendly." We thought: yeah, he'll definitely mete out justice for the hooligan pranks of the "Evil Empire." And, some years later, high above the Adirondacks, having descried a wing of U.S. Air Force planes, I thought, mockingly, for old times sake: "ours!" It was only natural that during this time Ronald Reagan became an idol of our group. Like Nikolay Rostov with the tsar in *War and Peace,* we fell in love with the American President. This feeling—in truth, rather jocose—more than irked American intellectuals who from time to time visited our circle, but in the heat of the moment we chalked their reaction up to snobbism and the "childish illness of the Left." (Now I wouldn't judge them that severely).

---

[2] In Moscow, there is a Progress Theater, a Peace Prospekt (Boulevard), and a Soviet Hotel.

[3] A well-known Russian writer.

To my taste, the best monument of the ancient game of bowing low before the West was the "Ode to the Seizure of St. Georges, October 25, 1983," written by Alexander Soprovsky, regarding the landing of American armies on the Island of Grenada. Due to lack of space I cite selected strophes and the final chord of this excellent poem:

> I drink a lot of vodka,
> And don't neglect port wine
> Even on an empty stomach.
> I grab the charming ladies,
> Now and then, in different places.

> And now in the White House
> You press against the morning news
> Democracy in stirrups,
> Not knowing other concerns
> Other than the rights of one man.

> . . .

> The dawn shines over the Potomac.
> Under the stars and stripes
> Of McDonald's, the victorious fleet
> Flies like a bird over a ravine,
> A predatory fish swimming—
> And lo! the bulwark of Marxism was falling.

> And over the waves of the Caribbean
> By the green of Manzanita
> The sons of an international power—
> O you, young MacFarlane,
> O you, intransigent Weinberger—
> Thunder to doomed Havana!

> For whom, amid wild drunkenness
> Do I sing, jumping from the table?
> Who, taking up arms against the powers of evil,
> Casting aside the Kremlin tanks?
> In whom has honor not yet died?
> Whose legendary dealings
> Will Yankees for ages never forget?
> The Californian eagle's!

The reality, as is its wont, did not hesitate to respond to the fantasy, taking everything subsequent unto itself. And, it must be noted, the author's fanciful fabrication was indeed phrased in keeping with the stylized genre, in the spirit of the adventurous eighteenth century.

We were overcome by the violent morning shakes—and a good third of a bottle of warm champagne foamed out, staining our hands, shirts and chins. Taking turns, straight from the bottle, we emptied a second and final one. And started to feel better. To mark the occasion, we set out aimlessly into the depths of Moscow. Only now did it catch our eye that the capital seemed dead, and only black government motorcades prowled here and there, turning on their flashing lights and chirps. "The satraps are out—and to hell with them," we decided and left Smolensky Square for the Arbat. We immediately fell into a crush of people. The crowd pitched from side to side exactly as if it were pursuing someone. Inside, the service personnel of the nearby cafés and restaurants in the formal old Russian headdresses and tall chef caps drew towards the windows of those eating establishments, flattening their noses from curiosity. Neither Soprovsky nor I for the life of us could understand what this ruckus was about, when the crowd suddenly exhaled a noise like a top-notch butcher. Here, into a stage-prop cabriolet of some enterprising street photographer in the middle of the Arbat, Nancy Reagan, first lady of America, lightly rose, and, in the next moment, the "California eagle"—the man himself—materialized. And we, in a comradely choir, with barbaric voices, through two armed cordons (an outer ring of

American thuggish mugs and an inner ring of Soviet), greeted the American President in horrendous English. And the next morning, we squabbled over a photograph in *Moscow News:* whose hand salutes in the right corner of the frame—the ode writer's or mine?

Fifteen years ago, societal events in our 1/6th of the globe began to develop with head-spinning rapidity, and already by the end of the 1980s I was hanging out in Montreal at the house of a second comrade from my youth. Together we dropped in on the local American consular office in order to straighten out our passports and roll into the "real America"—and visit a third buddy.

A white-haired black bureaucrat wearing inconceivable silver rings, who very much reminded me of someone else, gave me a blank questionnaire. Before I sat down to write, I strained to my memory . . . That's who! He reminded me of the Uncle Remus from the paperback cover—a North American version of Pushkin's nanny, Arina Rodionovna.

I took a liking to the questionnaire immediately, since it graphically confirmed to me the rightness of our circle's traditional native picture of the U.S. as a country where everything is topsy-turvy from ours. Answers, fraught with unpleasantness in the homeland, here were obviously welcome. I was a little annoyed that in the column "membership in the Communist organizations" I could only put a small expressive dash in place of a beautiful definition: "expelled because of personal convictions incompatible with being in the ranks of the All-Soviet Leninist Youth Communist League."

I was expelled in grand style—in a tall building in Lenin Hills at the committee meeting of the Youth Communist League of Moscow State University, equivalent to a district committee. But within a month or two of my public execution, I let my parents know that in place of a diploma I would get a scarlet letter, and they sounded the alarm. A friend of my parents, an invalid from the war, a violinist and director of a privileged music school, drank a bottle of cognac with the high-ranking daddy of one of his students, who softened the blow prepared for a freethinker by Soviet fate. Thus my banishment from the "ranks" ended without much of a bang, as one would like twenty years later, when filling out consular papers.

On the appointed day I came for the visa. With much disapproval Uncle

Remus extended to me my papers:

"You are allowed to enter the country, even though you concealed from us your affiliation with the Communist Party."

"How is that possible?"

"The computer showed it."

Alice in Wonderland, indeed.

In the morning, I, a freshly baked Bolshevik with a jar of beer in his hand, was pulling up in an express bus to the Canada-American border.

"If they get interested at passport control, whoever you are, don't get it in your head to characterize yourself as a 'poet,'" a Russian traveler warned me just in time, "they'll turn you away just like that: they have their own nutcases aplenty."

The officer of border service transferred his stern gaze from Mr. Gandlevsky's visage to his photo in the "hammer-and-sickle," then returned the passport. Uttering some inarticulate American sounds, he smacked the stamp down, and I found myself in America.

"I have never seen another country yet. The border held mystery for me. Ever since I was a child, I dreamt of traveling most of all." Pushkin . . . Yes, precisely.

They called us to board. Before climbing into the bus, I lingered in order to say my own dumb *howdy* to this unlikely America, and take a good look into the long-awaited foreign land. But visibility had suddenly worsened; a heavy snow was falling at an angle. Through an absolutely empty area to the control-admission point, a short file of people drew near. In front was a man in a long black coat and black bowler hat, and behind him, as if his copies, stood five boys, uniformly decreasing in a funhouse mirror, small-smaller-smallest, in little coats and bowler hats of the same unchildish cut and color. The wind mercilessly blew the sidelocks of the six.

Why were they wandering from country to country on foot? Was it a Saturday? In an overflow of emotion, I memorized this picture postcard of an exodus.

*Translated by Philip Metres*

# A REAL AMERICAN GIRL

## LINOR GORALIK

Steek your grincart up your ass. My perfikt hi-tek profeshin? Take it and hang in it, push your visa in your mausth—I don' need it. You think I want come to your Amerika, live in your Amerika, be immigrant in your very big, free, smoking-no, drugs everyver, many refugee Imperia Good you protect so good from bad people like we dreaming all time to take place in middle its big, soft, warm nyanya black tits? Oh you think I want be happy refugee and get my sitzenship in five years that's all, and not show my accent never, and tell my kits: "Bebe, mama and papa not Rusheen, they Rusheen-Ameri-keen!"? Bite me. Fuck you. I don't want any of these.

I want to be a pretty different thing—an American Girl, a real American Girl—but it's totally impossible, unreal, unthinkable—and not because I'm unable to mimicrate, to lose my accent ("Oh, oh, wait, your pronunciation . . . South New Jersey?"), to learn how to wear anything—from GAP clothes to a diamond necklace—with my sneakers, to drive a car, to tell a highway from a freeway, to give the finger. I can do all that, I can, I really can. It doesn't seem difficult to me. But: with your green card and my finger, with sneakers and dia-monds, with a car and no accent—I will never turn into a Real American Girl. I'll rather turn into the worst possible kind of immigrant—the frenzied "amerikos," spluttering while madly attacking a visiting Frenchman who dared complain about food quality in the local 7-11; the frenzied "amerikos" able to name all the Presidents one by one, next nearest, backward and forward; the pathetic citizen of a great country, who is languid with gratitude for the trust granted to him; the neurotic patriot making the locals shrink back guardedly: "Oh, these im-migrants, you know, sometimes they are so shocked by becoming Ameri-cans . . ." And I don't want any of these, I want to be a Real American Girl who reads carefully the one-hundred-dollar note and asks: *"Benjamin who? . . ."*[1]

---

[1] Words and sentences in italics appeared in English in the original Russian text. The rest was writ-ten in Russian.

I want something that neither a green card, nor language, not your little blue passport (I already have one little blue passport), nor the Fourth of July fireworks and hot dogs can grant me. I want my mother to give birth to me in *a Saint Louis hospital,* because all the women in my dad's family gave birth in *that Saint Louis hospital,* and I want my dad to watch me from behind the glass—sobbing, dropping his tears on his *New Yorker,* which he reads to distract himself from fear and to wash away the awful taste of *instant coffee.* I want my parents to bring me home in a car with huge, silver, *streamlined tail fins* and to put a little silver cross around my neck, one presented by my mom's *book club* at my *baby shower.* I want my first rattle to be a *Hello Kitty* with rolling eyes. I want to be moved from one kindergarten to another because their cook *is probably a fag.* I want to go to school and lose my thirty-two *Crayola Gold Medal School Crayons* on my first day there. I want to win my first-ever *spelling bee*—and to keep winning them all the way up to the nationals. I want to learn everything about menstruation from the *Joys of Menstruation* movie. I want to fall in love with a guy ten years older then me because he has a real *Harley* and looks like *Van Halen.* I want my unrequited love to make me start writing a diary in a special notepad with a real padlock and *"My Dear Diary!"* printed in pink at the top of every page. I want to exchange lunches with other kids and to be proud with my pretty *lunchbox* showing *Masters of the Universe* on the inner cover—a *non-metal* one. I want to have fights with my father because *Harvard is not good for girls.* I want to fear the pill because of that *Thalidomide* story. I want to distribute leaflets against *sexist male teachers* on my campus. I want to be hospitalized and be discharged *drug-free.* I want to love a man whose father was *lost in Vietnam.* I want to give birth while they are shouting *"Breathe! Breathe!"* and I want my husband to hold my hand. I want to work for my *mortgage.* I want my daughter to hurt her eye playing *Frisbee.* I want to find out my husband is having an *affair* with a shopgirl from *Barnes and Noble.* I want to start dieting and *to become anorexic* in three months. I want to be hospitalized and I want a shrink in the hospital to explain that *I simply don't love my husband anymore.* I want *to have an ugly divorce.* I want *to start really thinking about my career.* I want *to become a partner at the age of just thirty-three. I want to have breast cancer and write a book about all the nastiness of my chemical therapy—"for all*

*other women to know: they can make it!" I want to wear a pink ribbon on every and
each Kids Cancer Day and to donate one hundred dollars to Kids Cancer Organizations each and every year. I want to have a small, easy-to-solve tax problem. I want my
daughter to become a lesbian newspaper columnist. I want my second husband to be from
a real Richmond family. I want my son to lose a finger firing Fourth of July fireworks.
I want to lose all my savings due to the September 11 NASDAQ crash. I want to get it
all back with Chinese investments. I want my second son to find out he has AIDS and
jump from the Golden Gate Bridge, and his girlfriend to dedicate her life to staying
alive and managing a shelter for AIDS-infected people—in my son's loving memory.
I want my husband to come out of the closet at the age of sixty-nine. I want to start a
branch of the American Daughters of Liberty in my seniors retirement community. I
want to decide I believe in God two days before I die. I want to give my silver cross to
some kid visiting the hospital for his anatomy project. I want to go to my death praying
for my country. I want to be cremated in the Saint Louis Hospital.*

*And you can give me nothing of that. You can't give me such* a childhood, *and
you can't give me that* Christmas and a sock by the fireplace, *and Truth or Dare,
and* Batman when I could still believe in him, *and* real headbands for working out, and the belief that we have no villains that we can't destroy, and the
right to say: "We, Americans." So—stick your green card up your ass, hang
yourself on my perfect hi-tech profession, eat your working visa. Leave me living in the world, where money is green and salaries are "black." Where faces
have nationalities.[2] Where building number six can be eight miles away from
building number eight on the same street. Where my son is going to die at
the musical hall, poisoned by military gas.[3] Where there is four times the literature, three times a year, two times a day, one time a life.

And everyone wants to spend it in America.

*Translated by the author*

---

[2] In Russian, there is a bureaucratic cliché meaning person of an ethnic minority which literally says
"face of minor nationality." The words "face" and "person" have the same sound in Russian.
[3] In October 2002 more then 200 hostages were killed at the "Nord-Ost" (North-East) musical by
poisonous gas during a military operation aimed at releasing nearly a thousand hostages from the
building, which was occupied by terrorists.

# Goodbye, America. And—Hello!

## Olga Ilnitskaya

I'm sad today—I've never been in America. I've never seen how the New York freeways bend, "like a woman having an orgasm," and I'll never see how "the phalluses of the World Trade Center rest in the American sky. Now the American sky has terrorists that are mobile and elusive, like spermatozoa, and with whom it's necessary to contend. Because now, everywhere and always, there is war."

The erotica of the first paragraph is not accidental—it's the consequence of someone else's perception, for I don't have my own. And it is uncertain whether there will ever be my own, firsthand. Everyone says that it's difficult to obtain permission to go there—simply to fly in and check things out. You'll get tired explaining to everyone in the American embassy that it's only tits inside your bosom, not an explosive package.

But then it is known, that "a new interest is emerging in the present geopolitical and cultural situation of the United States of America—how the image of this country will form in the consciousness of foreigners."[1]

Clearly, I am the above-mentioned foreigner to these interested parties, but what are they to me?

Clearly, too, I am an antipode, *antidope,* by the very inner structuring of my head. And my "cultural consciousness" is rightfully different, so in my depiction—*in essay form,* of the image of a country where I *never was* and which I've *never seen*—I can be as unintelligible as I want to be. For it's pretty clear anyways that no normal American will ever understand me—if he/she is a real, true-blooded American, that is, and not, you know, one of the "formerly us."

American films are interesting to watch from an ethnographic stand-

---

[1] The quotation is from the letter sent by Dmitry Kuzmin to contributors soliciting them for this anthology.

point, with their long roads on which low, broad-assed cars speed with peo-ple in them. How and in what do they dress? Which color ranges do they prefer, in order to blend in and hide among the crowd, or, conversely, to boldly announce themselves to the world? Are they similar to us or . . . and one always gets stuck with this *OR* in the end! Either they're too handsome or too gangsterish, too black or red or yellow, and they all are just raring to go into battle for their lives—stubbornly and cheerfully, clambering over piles of corpses, with their lips stretched into that eternal "say-ch-eeeee-se." With their girls by their sides—oh, what super-beautiful girls! Beautiful, yes—but total airheads.

American boys and girls move . . . no, not just with a sense of com-plete freedom, lack of inhibition, but—with excessive looseness, that's how. Some even worse than that. Constantly they're chewing, drinking straight from a tin can, patting each other—on the shoulder, on the bum, on the jaw. Armed to the teeth—with all kinds of weapons: guns, brass-knuck-les, jagged necks of bottles, occasional dumbbells, ice picks. Lawn mowers, chain saws—weapons also! Cigarette lighters, too. The first people I ever saw being burned—Americans. They poured gas on them and set them on fire, like we used to do with pieces of wood on young-pioneer holidays. No, wrong, I forgot: the very first time I saw a burning human being was on the Soviet screen—it was in the year 1956, in the heroic film called *Al-exander Nevsky*. A warrior in a horned helmet—a Swede, I guess, or some such—threw a small girl into a bonfire. The biggest shock of my life. Now, in the year 2002, there are people burning every day, both in American and Russian movies—constantly, repulsively. No horror in that anymore—just a bad habit of watching those movies. I struggle with this habit, turn off the TV now and then. Wouldn't be a bad idea for them to re-introduce cen-sorship. Like in Soviet times. Not a political censorship—a psychological one.

I can imagine myself in Kansas City, in a checkered shirt, shit-stomp-ers and jeans with an undone zipper. My hair is unkempt forever, scattering in the wind, in my little knapsack: shampoo and condoms, my boyfriend's photo, a pilfered Faulkner, I'll forget it next to my little cup of coffee in

McDonald's. For that reason, from a random acquaintance I'll borrow *One Hundred Years of Solitude,* but it'll turn out that inside the dust cover, comics have been inserted instead of actual pages. The book's owner, you see, kept tearing the pages out to use instead of napkins, as he was finishing his own plastic cup of bad black coffee. Well, but at least there's plenty of coffee, the cup is tall, plus the hamburger.

One might get the impression I've never seen any normal American people. Well, rightly so. Never have. Nor any abnormal ones, either. I only saw Americans once, if you want to know—when they dropped in on a ship in the Odessa harbor. A friendly visit. And even then—oh, how I gazed upon them!—they were merely walking past! In their snow-white seaman's overalls. Or their little ironed officers shirts. Otherwise—where would I meet them, how? I'm not a black marketeer, not a prostitute, I don't serve in the diplomatic corps, I don't even work as a counter assistant in a faculty cafeteria where the vice-dean for international relations, my one-time admirer and college chum Vassily Vassilyevich, takes his meals. An ordinary, average, well-behaved woman, with the command of only one conversational language—how would I even be able to communicate and otherwise socialize with Americans? And as for my contacts with my former compatriots, who managed to get their American passports in exchange for years of emotional and physical overexertion, well, their version of the American experience, the view of America through the distorting glasses of the newly-converted—all that, I daresay, is of no interest to anybody. Even to me their stories are boring.

And I would dream of going there, of wandering around San Francisco, rolling on the lawn in the vicinity of some park in Los Angeles . . . To me it isn't really interesting to think about America in such a way that its image springs into existence. To me, it is interesting to think about concrete things: here, on this toy elephant calf, on his rear end, is an American flag. And my little son, a mere child as he is, already knows what's on the Americans' flag—the striped sky, and lots of stars. And ours was red, like blood. Now we have a different one, and he always confuses it with the Dutch flag. Quite understandably, America attracts him a great deal more, always has, because of that elephant with a flag on its rear end! Me, too! But—a one-sided attraction. In the sense that, you know, "none of me lives there yet, none was ever there." Didn't happen. And that which did not happen could not have happened. That's the way I see it. So far.

Yet I would indeed love to go there. To gaze about, to touch things, to get acquainted, to rejoice at the realization that nothing of that is true, what I've written here under the influence of American films, literature and other people's letters . . . and my own aberrations . . .

I would want to arrive and start with doing just that—saying goodbye, you see, to the America of other people's impressions—incorrect, stupid, beautiful or ugly. Goodbye!

And say with a broad smile: "Hello, my America! So this is what you're like!" But this would have been "before." And now, today, America is also . . .

This: "Anguish, terrorists, terror—where can one hide from them, is it even possible to hide, since they do exist, but how do you get used to . . . all this! All the more so that . . . to love and pity the victims of the terrorists is easy and only too natural, but, you see, these very terrorists (really, were they too not victims?) also need someone to love and pity them. And it looks like this someone is me. There's so much of everything in this whole thing, only it's better to be quiet about it for now." —This is from a letter from an American. One of the "formerly us."

This, too: "Yesterday evening . . . I returned from Florida, where I re-laxed-shmelaxed for a week. A gentle warm sea, similar to ours. Gentle warm air. Many palms and all sorts of subtropical trees and other plants. Pink flamingos, motionless little crocodiles, which seem quite peaceful, if not benevolent. And the people, who are quite serious about solving the problems involved in visiting the swimming pool, hairdresser, cosmetologist—they converse about the advantages of one beach relative to another, etc. Strange, no?"

Further: ". . . and I returned. The trip was nice, quite fine, everything would have been perfect, had it not been for . . . After all, this blasted 11th of September stirred up all kinds of human . . . ideas? fears? ways of life? At

first most people didn't really understand what happened. I myself, in re-
acting to someone's 'This might actually affect you. You might not be able
to fly out today'—replied cheerily: 'Ha. My flight's not until late at night.
By evening everything will have already been fixed and re-opened (meaning, the airport) a hundred times.' This was before the second explosion.
Then, after the third, a sense of horror started to creep in. After that, when
the plane crashed in Pennsylvania, we just all waited for what was to come
next. And still are waiting. Because—something is bound to happen, it feels
like. Life has really split into BEFORE and AFTER, though, of course, can
Soviet people really be surprised by horrors of any kind? Americans, they're
going through something like this for the first time, to them it's inconceivable, how such a thing could happen. On the other hand . . . In the morning, on the bus, the tour guide said to the group: 'In New York, for the time
being, there is nothing new. For the time being everything is quiet.'—and
everyone heard someone respond: 'In what sense?'

"To me, the gloating delight of some Russians was not surprising. Rather, what surprised me was the fact that the majority of Americans wanted
America to bomb Afghanistan. It doesn't surprise me that they're thirst-
ing for revenge, it's just that such a bombardment seems to me so obviously
senseless, even from the standpoint of revenge (all the same the wrong people will die), not to mention all the rest of it. Tomorrow, that is, on Mon-
day, I go back to work. Could've gone to California (tickets are very cheap
right now, and I've been invited). Could've tried going to Odessa, too, and
maybe even to Europe (don't catch me on my words, I know that Odessa is
also Europe). But somehow I don't feel like doing anything. And it seems
somewhat shameful now to travel, too. It's not the time. I'll postpone until
a better time. If such a time can be expected in the near future.

"Something happened to all of us, inside of us, after September 11th.
Incidentally, I just caught myself saying, for the first time—and twice—
'us' in relation with America. I shouldn't have gone to Canada, either. Even
though it's a wonderful country, and everything was just terrific. But . . .

"When I come back to my senses more, will write another letter, ok?
On December 11, 2002."

It hurts me to read this, think of what I'm reading . . . What did she have to go through, my "our American," in "their-our" America!

"Americans are very touching in their grief. They are, of course, all different, but they're unaccustomed to global tragedy on their own territory—they've maintained pure, childlike feelings and the astonishment of babies, for the first time recognizing that evil exists in the world, and that it can touch them.

"Two women on the fortieth floor carried a third woman who couldn't walk. Carried her all the way out to the street. All three survived. And I imagine to myself, how they went (it lasted more than an hour, probably) and not once did they hasten their steps, they didn't run, even knowing that it could be the end. Even though wisdom would suggest that they run as fast as possible. Because it would be better for the two to save themselves than to lose all three of them. Why add to the number of senseless fatalities, and so forth. Why then are we all so happy that they were so unwise?

"Waves of animosity stirred toward Arabs, and toward Jews, for good measure. ('If we hadn't been defending them, nothing would have happened.') More than eighty percent of average Americans, in response to a poll, said they would approve of the government if it would order the bombing of Afghanistan.

"Today was a day of mourning, and candlelight vigils took place all over the city, on the streets, by the houses, in the parks. They weren't official, nor mandated, but rather totally spontaneous, and everywhere. And candles were in the hands of passersby, too."

After *this* day, September 11, for all of us, American and non-American foreigners, America—bitter, bright, free, frightening, helpful and interested—became more comprehensible, and it became closer. Even more so than ever. How sad it is, that for so many it has only happened after *this* day.

*Translated by Andrea Gregovich*

# On American Culture

## Leonid Kostyukov

America is a land of fools.

In other words, America in general and American culture in particular are the most grandiose experiment in the history of mankind: what can a multitude of energetic fools do when they are together? An intelligent person should always keep an eye on America in order to know what he should not do.

Blok said: one should not call things that have a different name art. The sentence is witty but ambiguous. Many nerdy scholars attempted to give a definition to art, its purpose and functions, approaching it from the main door, from the positive side. The true result of their efforts proves that such positive definition is impossible. Whichever clearly formulated function or purpose you take as the major one, there is always proof to the contrary: non-art that performs the indicated function and achieves the above-mentioned purpose. Among such non-art that plays the role imposed on art by fools, mass culture takes a place that is far from insignificant. Its indicators are thrill and emotional impact; therefore, true art is related to these indicators but indirectly. Mass culture is a phenomenon that is primarily American in its spirit.

American mass culture targets American consumers. Their main features are: weakened associative thinking; a straightforward, unironic sense of humor; attention deficit; the desire to be like everybody else; treating art consumption as a routine business deal; confidence in the American way of life. For comparison, features of a Soviet consumer from the same viewpoint: powerful associative-parodying thinking; irony bordering on cynicism; strong nerves; attention to detail; an inner contradictory desire to be like everybody else and like nobody else simultaneously; treating art consumption as a potential deception; belief in the ludicrousness of the Soviet way of life in all of its manifestations with the exception of the main ones. It's hard to say whether mass culture has brought about mass consumption of art or the former has adjusted to the latter. Most probably, it went both ways: a mechanism of reciprocal linking has been formed, a stable self-correcting pair that is striving to the ideal of mass cultural service: an idiot with Down's Syndrome sitting in front of a TV screen on which a naked ass is fired at from the latest-model four-barrel gun. A naked ass is a special topic.

As a seagull has become the symbol of the Art Theatre,[1] a naked ass is Hollywood's trademark. The very simplicity of this apparatus rocks the ground under the feet of the vulgar post-Marxist art theoreticians. Really, what economic basis of the porno-film industry can one talk about? The above-mentioned ass and an amateur camcorder is all that is necessary for the shooting of a midrange porno movie. And if this kind of filmmaking does not grow roots in Russia, neither diplomatic smugglers nor the district Komsomol[2] Committees are to blame. It is just that cultures are different. In Russian culture, porno movies are taken as obscene anecdotes. The difference is obvious: the movie is literal while the anecdote is, for the most part, a phenomenon with subtext; porno films, above all, resemble each other while anecdotes are sort of freshly minted. Listening to a joke requires of a consumer much more talent than watching an (American) film. Let us go back to the characteristics of an ordinary American and check how these traits manifest themselves in the phenomenon of mass culture:

1. A consumer's weakened associative thinking allows the director (producer, writer, pop-group leader) not to be afraid of the following reaction from her/his viewer (listener, reader): "I have seen (heard, smelled) it somewhere already." Really, how can it be "it" if THERE the hero had a red shirt, while HERE it's light blue; if THERE he was chased by eighteen thugs, while HERE by only fourteen; if THAT group was standing on the left, while THIS is on the right? Hence the possibility of multiplying a successful bestseller or a song through "slight variations"; film stars resembling other, more famous film stars; groups of the Modern Talking[3] type. Let us note that not only the "body" of mass production, the batch, is not art; neither is what brings this batch to life.

---

[1] A famous theatre in Moscow where some of Chekhov's plays premiered.

[2] Youth Communist League.

[3] German pop-group, popular in the late '70s and early '80s.

2. An average American's sense of humor is on the level of the afternoon siesta in the young-pioneer camp (older groups excluded). Hence—a certain nostalgia for the American art, movies primarily: it is a chance to remember one's hectic, barefoot pre-acne childhood. Another, no less amazing impact of the American movie is that it is really funny. The figures of the director, scriptwriter, etc., decipherable behind the screen, are exceptionally funny. As a comedy, one is even tempted to regard the film creators as intelligent people who play the role of cretins and in this way achieve their goal. Everything is in its place after you watch a social, psychological thriller or a horror movie: they are as funny as comedies, and for exactly the same reasons. Ridiculousness is a common feature of mass culture, the Midas touch of sorts, a brand.

3. An American's much-too-malleable nervous system is a phenomenon familiar to chemical dependency experts. This phenomenon brings about entire genres of mass culture; horror movie (novel), for instance. We, comrades, think it funny, while they are scared. Of course, we also have horror movies (a stretch: any war movie; no stretch: *Vii*[4]), and they are much scarier than their overrated Western counterparts.

4. A short attention span brings to surface—through flexible double-sided mechanisms of the world of money—flabby proposition: no movie has anything happening on the periphery of the frame; the main conflict is clear; the secondary plane, secondary plotlines, etc. are absent: it is necessary to focus the consumer's attention on just one thing, and one cannot even dream about anything more challenging. Hence the transportation quality of a Western book: you can read it and, at the same time, remember at what point on your route you are, whether you have to get off soon, and—to top it all—participate, silently and passively, in a conversation that is conducted within earshot. The reading of an original English text involves at least struggling through the language (thank goodness!), whereas translations are consumed like wa-

---

[4] A movie adaptation of Nikolai Gogol's famous ghost story.

termelons. While watching the film, it is advisable to talk about something, otherwise time will seem wasted.

5. The desire to be like everybody else solves the problem of a positive hero. All of his heroism is concentrated in muscles and fighting/shooting/driving skills; that's the end of his exclusiveness. Inside—something very average.

6. Treating art consumption as a business deal is very important for understanding a clear genre structure of mass culture. The genre indication is the product's tag. In one called *Twelve Chairs*,[5] a detective novel, the American reader would painstakingly follow the progress of Ostap and Kisa's search, create combinations of her/his own, cross out the moves played and so on. If one called it a humorous novel, the American reader would laugh. If a life story—contemplate. The American is not taught to just read: what do you mean, *read?* Why? What for?

The system of search and promotion is so important in mass culture that it is nearly capable of replacing the latter. Ten minutes of film trailer almost exhaust the contents of the film. "Almost" stands for a purely quantitative difference. The quantity (amount of time, number of corpses and naked asses, decibels of the sound) of the given movie is also a medical, psychiatric category.

7. Confidence in the American way of life manifests itself in a certain metaphysical satiety that permeates even the most (seemingly) anti-American film. The thing is that whatever constitutes an infringement on the American justices is speedily taken care of by the 100% Americans themselves. It is as if someone tries to clean a chalkboard not with a wet rag, but by crossing out the writing in the same chalk. Chalk keeps adding rather than disappearing. Newton's Third Law: for every action there is an equal and opposite reaction. In the sphere of cultural practice this law is modified into compromise: an action calls forth a reaction. Sort of an existentialist vomitive reflex.

---

[5]  A satirical cult novel by Ilf and Petrov.

Geographically, America and its environs are home not only to mass culture, but also to an essentially anti-American branch of culture. It is Vonnegut, Pollack, a few other names—indeed, the number does not matter. There are several (non-Hegelian) degrees of negation: first, hatred, a colossal anti-charge; second, the same charge, already burnt-down, concentrated, *seeing,* when one skillful shot is enough for an opponent to collapse in dust; a sort of cold hatred, alienation. The third degree of negation is: forgetting during one's lifetime. It seems simple and easy, a roundabout way of excluding the other two; however, a lack of thinking is no substitute for forgetting: it is profanation. One must first remember well in order to correctly forget later. These are very Russian issues. When we apply them to America, let us admit that not a single American has achieved the third level of negation, of a little America in him/herself. Well, maybe it is unnecessary. The first level—a serious hatred on equal footing with your opponent—is impossible, ungrounded. One cannot seriously hate mass culture. In other words, a serious fight with clinical idiotism is a form of clinical idiotism. That is why the most anti-American culture is highly ironic and very precise; it is on the second level of negation of mass culture.

Fuel provides energy. It does not matter what the fuel used to be (quantity makes up for quality): a dinosaur, an oak tree, shit, an electron in motion. American and Russian existence, the lives of two superpowers provide enough fuel for an individual. Mass culture apologists are promoting true culture in the same way the Stalin cult or age-old lies promoted it in our country. The syntax of semi-educated commissars became the syntax of Platonov's *The Foundation Pit.* It is precisely in this sense that the phenomenon of mass culture deserves thorough investigation: as an element of life rather than part of culture proper.

America is a land of fools, which has created attractive conditions for an intelligent person.

*Translated by Olia Prokopenko*

# "Mew" instead of "Moo"

## Grigori Kruzhkov

*I should declare in a steady and powerful voice that the world itself is just a prolonged "mew," which has been fried and served to us instead of a noble "moo."*

—V. Khlebnikov

You ask me what America looks like? America looks like the Aegean Sea. In the West it is inhabited by tribes of bellicose Hollywood people. In the East there are trade cities of Phoenicians and New Yorkers. In the middle, there is a large Archipelago of universities and colleges, and boats of cunningly smart possessors with various educational degrees plying in between them. Islands differ. On this island you will find a wise Prospero, on the other island you will see Polyphem seeing nothing behind his flock of sheep; and in another place a forehead fight of uncompromising factions make such a noise that, oh, Lord, save me from this! However, only here is it possible for a humanitarian "to step by the sea with a solid foot,"[1] and all the rest is fluidity, mud, Thalassa and a play of nice but mysterious and unpredictable dolphins.

This strange country begins with a split of your personality. Not even a split but with a break-up along many crystal planes simultaneously—for example, the break-up into an adult and a kindergarten schoolchild, into someone who lacks knowledge and someone who asks questions. The experience proves that it is impossible to be completely smart while speaking a foreign language, because one loses the nuances. You can fry a chicken but you will never make it "to be fragrant." For such a fragrance you need to have an inherited sense of smell.

English is "mew" and Russian is "moo." The difference is enormous. Imagine an American waiter bringing your dish: he says, "Enjoy your meal"

---

[1] A quote from Pushkin's *Bronze Horseman*.

or just "Enjoy." If only he knew the storm of feelings this word invokes in the Russian soul!

> Enjoy, everything does pass!
> Either good or evil, Fate
> Metes out glee and grief to us,
> None too soon and none too late[2]

An interpreter-colleague will tell me that "enjoy" means simply: "We hope you find the food appetizing," and it is not worth breaking one's head over some semantic shade. I agree; however, just look at how differently various nationalities express this concept. French say "bon appetite," which means: "Have a good appetite, eat more, and have a bite of everything." Americans say, "Enjoy your meal"—that is: "Experience enjoyment." Russians say, "Eat to your health's content," because the very idea of enjoyment is alien to Russian life—healthfulness is more helpful to it.

Not long ago, the British government conducted an experiment in posting poetry in Moscow subway trains. The promotional materials for this experiment read as follows: "Enjoy poetry on the road." If a translator understood the matter, he would write: "Stock up with poetry on the road" (like one stocks up with snacks) or at least, "Please, read to your heart's content." I am sorry to say this, but we feel too shy to enjoy ourselves, much less enjoy ourselves on the subway.

As Valentin Berestov[3] remembers, before N. Y. Mandelshtam[4] would start teaching children languages, she would advise them, "In order to learn to speak English, you should forget all shame for a while. Bark! Bleat! Hiss! Stick your tongue out!"

This feeling of shame goes away, almost goes away, and a new intonation attaches to you (as an iron can attaches to a cat's tail). Finally, I also

---

[2]  From a famous Yevgeny Baratynsky poem.

[3]  A well known Soviet poet.

[4]  Nadezhda Yakovlevna, Mandelshtam's widow.

became fairly fluent in American English, but I myself know that what I acquired is not a true mastery of the language but rather a habit of making do with what I've got—whereas, while observing truly bilingual people, I could see that by switching a language, they immediately transform into a different role, acquire a different skin: quite a stunning bit of acting, if not downright witchcraft!

A fairly banal thing happened to me: here, abroad, I nearly became—no, not a patriot so much (patriots, democrats—these are political terms) as some type of "patriophile," a lover of Fatherland; I started to compare everything of *theirs* to *ours*—and ours ended up being better. There is a catch, though: the level of comparison, with which I lifted the cup of American being, measured that cup and found it wanting, needed a counterweight. The counterweight was "our" life, life in Russia, which I assumed to be a constant—while in Russia at the same time everything was changing as rapidly as in a kaleidoscope. (An old friend, living in Los Angeles, said to me on the phone: " 'Nostalgia' is not a spatial concept but a temporal one. We miss not past places, but past times.") In other words, as you can tell, I gradually started finding fault with Americans more and more: too pragmatic, you see, wingless, only worship the golden calf. Sure enough, my "old-country" upbringing had played a role in that, too. In the environment that I used to live in, the money factor was never taken too seriously. Those very words—"poverty-richness"—smacked of political-economics theory or, I don't know, Dickens. A sudden turn of life with its rough-hewn financial side forward became a surprising discovery for me in America. Money as a measure of all things. Even space and time, it turns out, don't depend on Einstein's formulations as they do on sums in dollars. The distance extends if you don't have money for a plane ticket; the time contracts drastically if you have to exchange huge chunks for the monthly payments on the roof over your head. "And what do you do *for rent?*" (That is, how do you earn money to pay for an apartment?)—is a usual question of New Yorkers, when getting acquainted with each other. Robert Frost has a poem "Provide, Provide," which is very powerful, but is still untranslated into Russian—maybe precisely because of an unusual subject it touches upon. Can anyone imagine a Russian classical poem with a title like this? One could, perhaps, but only with difficulty. Pushkin came the closest to it in his "Conversation of a Bookseller with a Poet." And in his "The Covetous Knight." Would only he were just to toss aside the Baron's mask he wears in it and address the reader directly: "Provide, provide!"

I fell in love with Robert Frost a long time ago, by reading Andrey Sergeyev's[5] translations. Later I began to read him in English, and to translate. Recently I took a great interest in Frost's contemporary and countryman Wallace Stevens, who was a refined poet and an heir of English Romanticists and French Decadents. He spent all his life working in insurance and didn't have any financial problems in his old age. His *modus vivendi* affected me so much that I wrote a poem:

Wallace Stevens,

or

About the Appointment of a Poet
to the Position of Vice-President at an Insurance Company

Poems can't guarantee you anything. Chatterton,
stumbling, returns to his windowless attic pad,
jots off a note, gulps down arsenic. Mr. Poe
hardly rakes in a quarter per single line.
He's already finished depicting the cheese-loving Crow,[6]
Crane is up next, palm-sized Titmouse[7] he keeps in mind.
Pushkin writes debts in a column on poem's draft,
Adducing to it a coded new poem of sorts.
Steadily grows this poem from month to month.
One goes to trade in Africa; someone else
Chances upon a cheap used overcoat in Rostov.
There you have it—quite a nice little outfit. You can name

---

[5] 1933-97, a preeminent Soviet translator of English and American poetry.

[6] "Crow and Cheese" is the title of a famous Russia fable written by I.A. Krylov.

[7] "Better to have a titmouse in the palm of your hand than the crane in the sky"—a Russian saying.

This company Insure Your Life—sure, why not?
The judge asks: Who gave you the authority?—The
Board of Directors, the poet quietly but firmly replies.[8]
An excellent group of people: Goethe, Princess Badralbadur
and Mr. Stevens. Insurance against fire, war
and the end of the word. This is not the end of the world.
Why? Because in each minuscule morsel of frost,
*A priori,* forever dwells eye-canthus' crystal. Snow dust
slowly falls off the top of a tall northern pine.
A lonesome palm at earth's edge pines for a reply no more
Than that summer-besotted nightingale of the childish old
Russian saw.[9]

And what about the American poetry of today? I've looked at it for a good, long while—and, as you can imagine, with not a small amount of vested interest. Well, what can I say? A monstrous *ideological subterfuge* has taken place here—like, you know, back in our *sotzrealism* days; and let me report to you, incidentally, that this capitalist political correctness doesn't give an inch of ground to the Marxist dogma of our youth. Creative Writing departments (here, that is, the local Literary Institute[10]) post fliers of scores of poetic competitions: most often, what's needed in every instance is just doggerel on a given topic—something utilitarian and well within the bounds of an average *kolkhoznik*'s reason. The prestige of poetry has dropped to zero. Some graduate students in the Humanities openly admit that they simply *do not understand* poetry (not specifically Russian poetry, but poetry in general)—and these, come to think of it, are the would-be contenders for college-level teaching positions! So it's

---

[8] A reference to the exchange at Brodsky's trial in '64. The judge: "Who gave you the authority to call yourself a poet?" Brodsky: "No one. Who gave me the authority to enter the human race?"

[9] A pun on the subject of the poorly-educated Russians' characteristic sign off at the end of their love correspondence: "Zhdu otveta, kak solovei leta."

[10] Moscow Literary Institute: the only institution of higher learning in the USSR, and in Russia still, where creative writing is taught.

okay then, doesn't affect their professional fitness! You can only imagine what these future professors of literature will teach—and already are teaching—their students.

All of this didn't start yesterday. Back in 1579 the English puritanical writer Stephen Gosson published a treatise called "The School of Abuse," which was aimed against poets and "other parasites of the society." In response to it, Sir Philip Sidney wrote his "Defense of Poesy," where he pointed out that if God indeed created man to His likeness, and lifted man above all creatures, then a poet is a man who is more keenly attuned to the power of God's breath than are all of his brethren, someone capable of forging a "second nature," creating the works which equal or even surpass nature's doings: "Nature never set forth the earth in so rich a tapestry as divers poets have done . . . Her world is brazen, the poets only deliver a golden." But who will believe in it now? In America I encountered precious few people who genuinely understood poetry: the majority of them belonged to the margins of American society. As for the academic circles, strange things happen there. In poetry (and in literature in general), they only look for a reflection of some *social processes*—or some *physiological* processes, as the case may be—or any other processes—just not for a process of poetry, not one of arts. This disease is not specifically American in its nature; but in the pragmatic, puritanically minded America the seed sure did fall into a receptive soil.

In the year of 1819, John Keats, by that time sick and in despair, wrote the following, upon receiving bad news from his brother who emigrated to America:

> Where shall I learn to get my peace again?
> To banish thoughts of that most hateful land,
> Dungeoner of my friends, that wicked strand
> Where they were wreck'd and live a wrecked life;
> That monstrous region, whose dull rivers pour
> Ever from their sordid urns unto the shore,
> Unown'd of any weedy-haired gods;

Whose winds, all zephyrless, hold scourging rods,
Iced in the great lakes, to afflict mankind;
Whose rank-grown forests, frosted, black, and blind,
Would fright a Dryad; whose harsh herbag'd meads
Make lean and lank the starv'd ox while he feeds;
There flowers have no scent, birds no sweet song,
And great unerring Nature once seems wrong.

Almost everything here is a poetic exaggeration. The place isn't that evil, the ox is not quite so lean lank and starv'd, flowers do have scent, birds do sing. But Keats is right in one thing: weedy-haired gods don't inhabit American rivers. No Dryads, or Nereids, or even common mermaids, at the very least, have ever been observed there. This is a Country of Future, not of Past.

And the matter isn't only one of advanced technologies. In America (albeit not only in it) a giant experiment is being conducted in regards with mixing various ethnic groups into one new mega-entity. This process is accompanied by much enrichment—but it also results in horrific simplification: a language of culture turns into a Language of Contact Establishment (LACE). The mechanism of such a transformation is the same everywhere. "Me you gift soon give." It cannot be denied that this leads to the emergence of an interesting new expressivity; but unfortunately, it is no longer possible to explain to a person who speaks such a LACE what the phrase "The flying wrack of clouds grows flimsier far"[11] means.

Anything that is too complicated in LACE falls off by itself. Paradox, but this serves to accelerate the bureaucratization of the society, increases the power of a "piece of paper." That apocryphal "piece of paper" is considered an instrument of democracy in America, helping to even out opportunities for people of different origin and education. For the past fifteen years streams of "pieces of paper" circulating in the U.S. increased fifteen-fold. This alone brings down the value of any printed page. Plus, there are printed advertisements. If you receive in your mail daily five to seven letters, half of

---

[11] Pushkin, as translated by Avril Pyman.

which you throw into the trash without even opening them, then how does that affect the very sacred idea of *writing*—in both senses of this word?

Many people believe that great poets no longer exist, will never exist again—and cannot exist as a matter of principle. I won't argue with this. I just would like to remind you that Chesterton was saying almost exactly the same in the beginning of the twentieth century, at the time when a new Pleiad of European geniuses was already beginning to come into its own. And frankly speaking, did we and our time ('60s–'80s) really deserve such a poet as Brodsky? It didn't turn out according to logic, you see, but only according to God's will.

To me, the acquaintance with Brodsky, my very few meetings with him, constitute my most important American memories. America without Brodsky is a different country, not the one to which I came for the first time ("mew" instead of "moo"). And that's not only due to his poetry as such. Brodsky was a reminder of a true value of life, and to a larger extent than the giant ecumenical St. John's cathedral in New York, in which Brodsky's eulogy was held. He just wouldn't bring the stock of poetry down by selling it short; thus, the sheer weight of gold which is stored in the basement of the National Bank keeps the country from inflation.

I must say I strongly started to respect Mark Strand, who said during his talk at Columbia University (getting the audience to smile), "Iosif and I often called each other, read poems to each other and asked each other for advice. You can conclude by one detail how much better he was than me: I always followed his advice, but he never followed mine."

*Translated by Julia Mikhailova*

# A Poem about a Canadian Passport

## Artur Kudashev

By the way, there is absolutely no poetry in this piece. It will be in prose, and although Canada and a passport will be mentioned, this prose is about the USA. I heard somewhere that if a piece does not have an enticing title, then no one will ever read it. Especially if the subject is hackneyed, like one's impressions on a trip to America. The public dismisses such essays with disdain: "Oh, we've read *that!*" Yes, of course you've read that, but I, for one, haven't yet written about it!

So, before you are notes about foreign lands. And America is the ultimate foreign land among all other foreign lands. I remember on coming off the flight from New York and entering the metro station *Rechnoi vokzal* I experienced an overpowering desire to grab the first person I came across on the escalator by the lapels and yell: "Do you know, you and your stupid mug, where I've just been?" Now time has passed; I thought the passion had subsided, but it is still there and there's something hard and cruel about it. You know I feel like sharing my experience. Only what am I to call all of this? "My Very Own Discovery of America"? "Among the Cities of the Yellow Devil"? "The Brand-New American"? "Don't Steal (From a Classic)"?—one ought to write prominently among the textbook do's. But where would we be now, our ultra-modernist, nonfat and vegetarian selves, without stealing from the classical writers?! Well, what of it? They have a hell of a lot of material. Especially Mayakovsky, especially since he was in the USA. The title, "A Poem about a Canadian Passport," has another meaning, probably not very deep, but fairly advanced—all the way at the very end of this essay.

## The Grants of General Grant

That's what I wanted to title my composition in the beginning. Then I changed my mind. I also changed my mind about why it is that Americans use their own money to bring over foreigners. I changed my mind about a lot of things. Where the American government is concerned, everything is pretty much clear. That's how it introduces selected aliens to its system of life, and this is a better and possibly the cheapest way of making friends, which America needs more and more of. But what this does for the common taxpayers, in whose families the aliens live during the term of their grant, is unclear. They don't receive any benefit or subsidy for this, and the last thing they need is to let into their home a stranger who has not been tested for syphilis and has not been examined for pediculosis. What they say is that they're curious—that's how they get to know the wide world.

Traveling to America cannot *not* change your life. This is a point of new beginning. Before this moment you know the world insufficiently in the extreme, but after—oh, so sufficient that it begins to seem that nothing better than that will ever happen to you. I remember one *Perestroika*-era television program in which inquisitive TV reporters took a bum off the streets, washed him, clothed him, put shoes on his feet, fed him at a good restaurant, and after that the show ended. The journalists made their segment, went off on new business, but the bum, clean and fed, was left where they had picked him up. I remembered his eyes at that moment.

There is something similar about a trip to the USA. For a month you are shown a kind of life that really does exist on our planet—reasonable in the literal sense of the word and happy for everyone who desires it. And then it's over. The picture is extinguished, and you end up in the same place you were sitting before the screen lit up. And all around you once again are the sullen faces of your countrymen, getting up from their seats and heading for the theater exit, coughing and hurrying to use the john. "Just a minute!" you want to yell in that instant, "Just a minute! What about me? I, who now knows for sure that all of this exists on earth? I want that too!"

And so . . . But enough about sad things. Better to write about happy things. Of the eight people making up our group, after returning home seven decided to leave Russia forever.

### Country of Airplanes

If Germany is, as they say, the country of cars, then the USA is the country of airplanes. Although it is, in principle, the country of anything—but especially of airplanes. Americans are fervent supporters of air travel. The route of our travels looked like this: from Moscow to New York, then a transfer to a flight to Detroit, where we again transferred to another flight, to the city of Kalamazoo, our destination. By car you can get here from Detroit in two hours, but air travel, including the time spent on registration, waiting to board, etc., takes about three. If we add to this the cost, then clearly the scales tip in favor of the automobile. In defiance of this fact, the bright red little Northwest airplane flew off completely packed with passengers.

There are a lot of funny things about American airplanes and airports. When they batten down the entrance before takeoff, the stewardess walks down the rows and asks each passenger: "To Detroit? . . . To Detroit? . . . To Detroit? . . ." This is what is meant by "foolproof." In airports practically at every step you can find genuine thrones on which old blacks sleep sitting up. These are the shoe shiners at their work stations. Strangely enough, in airline work there's a lot of chaos. For example, due to the strike of "our" airline, on one of the legs we flew in a "strike-breaker" airplane. Because of this, during the transfer of the ticket I had to pay an additional hundred dollars out of my own pocket, due to the attendants' mistake. But I give credit to American methodicalness and honesty: a month after my return to Russia I was sent that hundred back with an apology and an invitation to fly only Delta in the future.

I promised to think about it.

When we approached Kalamazoo, it was already the dead of night. As we were descending, at some moment two bright stripes of light became visible beneath us, one white, the other red. They both started on one side of the horizon and ended on the other side. For a long time it wasn't clear what this was, until one of us figured out that this was the flow of cars on the highway, speeding along in one direction and the other. This is an unobtrusive demonstration of the might of the American economy. So don't believe those TV reporters about the crisis of the dollar and so on. They claim the West rots, but the actual scent is excellent as usual.

But I don't want to tell you about Kalamazoo at all. It's a cool place, what can I say?

## Shkago-on-Mishkan

The strong Michigan-Illinois accent, besides "yup!" and "nope!" sounds like hissing to the listener. Here they say: "Mishigan," "Shicago."

I loved "Shicago" right away and forever. But nothing else is possible. In the same way I selflessly fell in love in the long-past 1983 with Tashkent—the capital of Central Asia, the model city of the communist future—when I arrived there for winter vacation with my class. I didn't require much back then!

Chicago is a feast of a city—no, not a moveable feast (see, you guessed wrong), but a feast of wind, light, water, concrete and glass. Not New York but Chicago, standing on the bank of enormous Lake Michigan, is the feast. Its horizon line with its three peaks of capitalism—the towers of Sears, Amoco and Hancock—will now constantly call out to me. The only thing that could be better is mountains. Probably . . .

It's unlikely that you'd be interested in an enumeration of all kinds of geographic and historical details about the "city on the lake," such as the fact that located here is the world's largest warehouse store or a magnificent dolphin park. Come and see for yourself.

It's better if I tell you a little anecdote. My neighbor in the hotel, Andrei, and I set out one evening on Michigan Avenue in search of entertainment. Our attention was attracted by a sign hanging on one of the street poles. "Welcome to American Girls Show!" it invited. And right there an address was printed in italics. It turned out that the show was being put on nearby. Andrei and I looked at each other. "We have to go!" he said. "Absolutely!" I agreed, and we dashed off to the "den of iniquity." We bought our tickets, entered the auditorium, sat down, waited.

Semi-darkness. The curtain had not yet been raised. We felt that something was amiss. We looked from side to side. The audience around us was composed entirely of middle-aged women and young school girls. Besides us, there was not a single man. What's going on? we thought. Then the curtain parted and eight twelve-year-old girls jumped out onto the proscenium and began to sing in unison. It turned out we ended up at a "show" of American school girls, not show girls! It was something in the vein of our TV show in Russia, "Morning Star." What a disaster!

Getting up and leaving would have been awkward, as we were sitting practically in the very center. And in the end, a musical performed by children appealed to us. It was a genuinely professional production. And we no longer regretted spending the money.

Among other things, in Chicago we went on a tour of the Stock Exchange. Impressions were mixed. A hybrid made up of the heart of the world and an insane asylum.

## Motor City-Brother City

In Togliatti[1] one can hear Italy, and in Detroit France. But no, alas—you can't find either in either place. But on the other hand, Togliatti has Azerbaijani and factory mafia, and Detroit—Greeks and Black Panthers. Or used to have, to be more precise. Both places still have decent hockey teams. And finally, Togliatti is an arm's reach from Tatarstan, and from Detroit you can see Canada. It's on the opposite bank of the river.

Overall, Detroit is quite a dreary city. It has its own business district, "downtown," with the usual skyscrapers, with various Renaissance centers and Cadillac towers, with monorail trains and an ultra-contemporary hockey stadium. But here it is neither comfortable nor good for the soul—in short, it's not as good as Chicago.

American friends have told me that Detroit is a city they dislike. The dislike started in the sixties, when dark-skinned Trotskyite-Maoists picked this location for testing out their power. Then the leftist hoodlums came out into the streets with Molotov cocktails and pieces of cement, and there

---

[1] A city on the Bolga River known as the center of the Russian automobile industry.

began massive prolonged disturbances in the city that ended with big business moving further away from the troubled Detroit. Its skyscrapers were emptied and still stand empty to this day. They look especially gloomy at dusk, when they resemble man-made, uninhabited mountains. Matters became even worse in the seventies, when Americans lost the small car war to Japan, and the motor city lost not only its head but also its legs—the factories—and I don't even know how many of them it had.

In present-day Detroit there are only two places that are more or less bubbling with activity. This is the section of Greektown, which is full of casinos and restaurants and a new baseball stadium. We were there and watched a baseball game. The game is interesting but incomprehensible the first time around. And the stadium's size is staggering. I understand how the vandals felt when they first got into the Coliseum.

In the stadium everyone eats. On every level there's a place where a pair of little spigots stick out of the wall—one with a red label and the other with a brown one. "For washing hands, maybe?" I thought. But no. Ketchup comes out of the red spigot, and out of the brown one—mustard.

The evening before I was to leave Detroit, my American friends suggested that we take a drive to get a peek of Canada. To do this you only have to drive through a tunnel under the river. So we went. At the immigration checkpoint a Canadian official told us, with an offended expression, that Canada is an independent nation and that a visa is required to enter its territory. We shrugged and said that we didn't know about this. But returning to the USA turned out to be not that simple—we had to wait for official paperwork from the Canadian Immigration Service attesting to the fact that we had been denied entrance. We had to wait as long as fifteen minutes. During all this time we studied Canada. And there isn't a damn thing of interest there. Only the signs are written in French as well as English, and the distances are written not in miles, but in my native kilometers.

## The Biggest Apple in the World

New York does not look like the USA. It reminded me of Moscow; someone else in our group thought it looked like Baku.[2] We, arriving from Russia, blended into New York better than many of our Kalamazoo acquaintances. And not only did we look like we fit in—we felt that way too.

Having settled ourselves into a hostel, we went out on the street and began to memorize, speaking aloud, the map of river ferry routes on the Hudson.

"Hey you guys!" the driver of a big bus standing at the entrance of the hostel shouted at us in half-Russian after about two minutes, "I'm going to 42nd now! If you want I'll give you a lift!"

We were speechless from the sheer unexpectedness of it, but quickly boarded the bus.

The bus began to move forward swiftly. The driver was silent, as though he didn't realize that he had made such a strong impression on us.

"How much will it be?" we asked him timidly.

"It's nothing!" he said dismissively, "Countrymen, after all . . ."

He was called on the radio.

"Gesha, where are you?" asked a hoarse voice.

"I'm exiting 73rd onto Broadway and going down!" answered our driver.

"There's a funeral going on somewhere in the thirties. Can you drop by?"

"Okay!" answered Gesha, "But first I'm going to 42nd."

"Got it!" the voice concluded, "Call when you can!"

In this manner we arrived at the Hudson pier. In the day remaining before our flight back to Moscow we managed to see a lot. The famous statue, Wall Street, Broadway, Central Park, the subway, and even a little piece of Harlem. In New York you quickly begin to feel right at home.

Americans call this city "The Big Apple." I think I understand how the biggest apple in the world differs from all others. Anyone can take a bite out of it. And there is yet one more New York subject that cannot in any way be avoided.

That the WTC no longer exists I cannot entirely believe—just as in the

---

[2] The capital of Azerbaijan.

past I could not entirely believe that it existed. But back then it definitely did exist, and now it definitely does not. Total insanity—both before and after.

I was even inside of it, on the first floor of the south tower. The line for the elevator to get to the observation deck was too long, and I turned and left. I thought: "Another time!" I exited onto the plaza between the two towers and from a Russian-speaking vendor bought a T-shirt with writing that said "I love this city" and a set of postcards showing local sights.

"Are 'the twins' in here?" I asked, going through the postcards.

"These, you mean?" asked the vendor, "Naw! What the hell do you want with those?"

"What of it?" I shrugged, suddenly feeling lonely.

The vendor grinned and was distracted. Some other people had walked up to him.

## Super-Papooses

I thought for a long time about what kind of word "amerikos"[3] is. Where did such nonsense come from? Why does any old schmo calmly call the citizens of the greatest country in the world this way? This has in it something of the giggling of teenagers about an oversized klutz of a classmate, who incidentally has enough strength to smear his peers on the wall. But he doesn't smear them. He has principles. And he is kind. So he'll give a flick from time to time or a kick in the ass if you get too close.

It's interesting that the word *native* is so applicable to Americans. They are natives, the most genuine kind of natives. Similar to those who came out of the forest to meet Columbus. They had smiles, gold and bananas. And the Spaniards had rum, syphilis and muskets. Luckily, for contemporary Americans a meeting with foreigners has become less dangerous. But its essence has not changed. They greet you with heart and soul, but those arriving—some come with this, some with that . . . but at a minimum they have their sights set on immigrating. So that from simple papooses Americans have evolved, I

---

[3] A denigration used commonly in Russia.

would say, into super-papooses.

And in the word *native* I hear this: "someone who is master of one's country." I am not a master of my own country—I don't feel that way. And around me I don't see people who do. Maybe the mafia are masters? Or those who reach cabinet level? Oh, just drop it . . .

### Native Medicine

I learned one thing about medicine in the USA: that in Russia there is no medicine. That which does exist is not medicine but rather a skeleton on a stick. Excuse me, but when I write on this subject I begin to choke on my own saliva like a doctor. And my saliva is of no use to you.

In a month's time I saw a lot, thanks to my American friends. I went to a private acupuncturist, and a chiropractor, and a Catholic hospital, and a Protestant one, and to a state madhouse where epileptics walk around decked out in hockey helmets (a very clever idea, I must say), and to a special clinic where anyone willing can receive a small shot glass of pink—no, not muscatel, but methadone—and to a meeting of underage drug addicts, and to one secret location, where I fraternized with a group of anonymous Kalamazoo alcoholics led by an Assiniboin Indian who looked remarkably like a representative for a union of southern Ural tribes, and also like a supervisory professor on the psychology faculty of Western Michigan University (psychology, it turns out, is "taught" and not "learned"—can you believe it?), etc., etc. . . .

Good job, Americans. I have no words. That is, I have words, but they're all somehow pitiful, inadequate: really cool, dude. For the first time in my life I understood what status I could have reached had my parents given birth to me in America. With the same amount of education and experience as I had in that other country, in this country I would have earned (God help me!) somewhere in the neighborhood of two-hundred-thousand dollars a year, and my friends, now alcoholic Soviet surgeons and anesthesiologists, would have made in the neighborhood of "four hundred," "five hundred," "six hundred" . . .

That's all—I don't want to talk about this anymore.

## Me Speak English Language

Overcoming the language barrier begins with the barrier of sounds. In the beginning the sounds of English speech sound like the chirping of birds. Then suddenly something turns on in the brain. "Chirp-chirpety"—this, it turns out, is actually, "Come this way, please," and "Chirpety-chirp" is, "Tea and coffee are available in the corner." And so on. And you understand everything. Probably in the same way that Dorothy from *The Wizard of Oz,* finding herself in a magic country, catches herself thinking that she can understand everything that her little dog says.

And then you yourself begin to chirp. In the beginning with uncertainty, breaking your beak on the words. But people understand you anyway! And then you're already yakking away with full force! And all by itself your speech comes out not on the wretched and endless topic, "I was born in . . . "—but on something much more digestible for the local listeners.

The remainder of the language barrier breaks down during sleep. At the end of my second week of life in the USA I found myself having dreams that were no longer in Russian.

The next day at dinner my American friends discussed the amusing accent of one of their English acquaintances. Later I had the opportunity to socialize with him. His accent really is awful . . .

## My American Friends

Every time that I now see some pink, well-fed wise guy on Russian TV cheerfully preach something about the threat of American expansionism, I think about Michelle with her daughter in her arms, or about Russel, climbing under a table in search of a computer disk.

In the States I met and became friends with many people, but most often I remember Michelle and Russel. Michelle is the owner of a small agency that specializes in rehabilitating alcoholics and drug addicts. Russel is a psychiatrist who works at this agency. When I first saw them at the reception in honor of our arrival in Kalamazoo, I didn't like them. Michelle seemed to me to be especially fussy—someone who smiled much more often than necessary, and Russel I simply didn't take seriously. I had already socialized with the local doctors, and not one of them had been pockmarked or wore a little braid despite the presence of an already sizable bald spot on his head or ridiculous sandals on otherwise bare feet. I knew from my schedule that I would be spending a whole four days in their office, and I prepared myself in advance for this to be nothing more than a chance for me to practice English conversation.

But everything turned out otherwise. You live for a lifetime, you learn for a lifetime. Michelle's daughter Julie turned exactly one month the moment we met. Once I held her in my arms while her mother sorted things out (by gesticulating and writing at the same time) with the parents of one young cocaine addict. Michelle met with clients and at the same time nursed her daughter, covering her breast with a big flowery kerchief. And Russel didn't give a damn about how he looked. And his clients also didn't give a damn. Because he was simply a first-class communicator and specialist. There is no reason to be surprised at this, for Russel graduated medical school with distinction, not just anywhere, but from Yale University.

Michelle and Russel watched over me, even after my scheduled four days passed. No one forced them to do this. The others, by the way, didn't do this—I was just lucky. Those are the kind of people they turned out to be—efficient and thoughtful. Before my departure Michelle gave me the gift of a wonderful trip to Lake Michigan, and Russel gave me a pile of things, two of which can now always be found on my work table: a small pitcher made of Vermont malachite and an NHL souvenir puck.

From time to time we exchange messages on the Net. They're very similar to the exchange of news between people who are hospitalized, and the topic of conversation is those who are not ill. "While rafting in Alaska I injured my arm . . . Ken and Raquel have flown off to Acapulco . . . There's no news from Maureen in Bamako for the second week . . ." and so on. I don't know what to write in reply. "They've raised the bus fare to seven rubles . . . I've retrieved my shoes from the repair shop . . . 'Ramstore'[4] has issued a discount card . . ."

---

[4]   A chain of supermarkets in Russia.

Michelle regularly sends me selections of American jokes. They're beginning to be funny . . .

## For Our and Your Canada!

This happened on one of the last days of my stay in the USA.

It was getting on towards evening. The three of us were sitting on a little balcony, slowly drinking Sterlitamak vodka, "Lux." Two of my new Canadian acquaintances: Peruvian Masha and Russian Dima, and one Russian resident—me, the Tatar. Dima and Masha are husband and wife and work in the States—she doing a residency in psychiatry, and he is in computers.

The barbecue was ready—pork, turkey, potatoes and corn. We began to eat.

"Forgive me," Dima suddenly said, "but I just want to ask. What on God's green earth are you doing living there, huh?'

I opened my mouth to answer, but Dima continued his question.

"No, explain this to me! What, you love the birch trees or something, huh? Well, there are birches here! There they are!" he waved his hand at the landscape, "I just want to understand—why do you live there? Why?"

I closed my mouth. Then I opened it, but only for the sake of taking a drink. There was nothing to say.

And in the meantime Dima continued.

"The whole country's bound to oil and war! The country's run by thieves! Only the mafia lives well! And the people—they're like brutes! Yesterday I watched the news hour on satellite dish—we can get it here. This is freaking nuts, man! Freaking nuts! And you're a doctor! A doctor! Have you seen how doctors live here?"

I nodded.

"And have you seen where they're all from? Have you seen? Half of them are Hindu and Pakistani. The rest are Czechs, Macedonians and Argentineans. Anglo-Saxons don't really go into medicine—you have to study for a long time, and money can be made in other ways. You understand? What does this mean? Huh? This means that you have a chance! A real chance for a real life for a human being!"

The Peruvian Masha put her hand on her husband's shoulder.

"That's enough, Dima!" she said in Russian, but with a mild accent, "He can see everything for himself. He will understand for himself what he needs."

Dima fell silent and waved his hand. We finished off our drinks and food and began to make our goodbyes. My American friends had already come for me.

"You think about it all the same," Dima said to me at parting. "Think about who you want to be in this life!"

"OK!" I promised.

"We will help you!" Masha spoke up unexpectedly, "We'll tell you what and how. It's hard, but possible. Of course getting into the USA is very complicated. But now, Canada—that's entirely possible. And there's no particular difference between them—this is all one free world. You'll be able to do this if you genuinely want it. After all, *we* did it! But the main thing is for you to decide—think about if you really want it . . ."

## A Poem about a Canadian Passport

Time passed . . .

Dear Masha and Dima!

I gave it some thought and decided . . .

But actually I did this almost immediately.

Yes, I want to be a Canadian. For a long time now. It is only natural. And not because life is easier there than it is here. Not because every Canadian is guaranteed a pension of five hundred bucks. Not because medical care there is free and high-quality. Not because a Canadian passport gives you the right to move all over the world without a visa.

I want to be a Canadian because . . .

Because I want to be in the avant-garde of progressive humankind. I am not kidding or being sarcastic. I want to go there. Nothing more, nothing less. Before, the Young Communist League, Komsomol was that kind of avant-garde. Now, it's the USA and Canada. It is exactly the avant-garde. And to get in there is even an exam, similar to the Komsomol exam in the past. All that's left is to clarify, for the sake of passing the exam, how many medals Canada has and whether it has democratic centralism.

America, my friends, is our common property, the property of all intelligent, thinking human beings. And cosmopolitanism is the newest patriotism, the patriotism of inhabitants of the planet Earth. And Earth, Vladimir Vladimirovich (Mayakovsky), is already "without Russias, without Latvias." We've lived to see it—can you imagine?

And it is so big. Much bigger than all of my troubles.

*Translated by Yelizaveta P. Renfro*

# LUXEMBOURG

## DMITRY KUZMIN

I must confess that America never excited me. I never really wanted to see the skyscrapers or the Grand Canyon—I was always more drawn to Europe, with its Gothic cathedrals and narrow lanes paved with cobble-stones. I grew up in a superpower country, whose expanses and ambitions aroused in me a deep irritation, and for this reason I was completely not attracted to another superpower with its own expanses and ambitions—I dreamed of Denmark and Luxembourg. To this day I believe that countries should be small, on scale with the life of a private individual—and then the needs and hopes of this individual in a natural way will take their rightful place at the forefront of his life.

I was lucky: no one from my inner circle went to seek his fortune on the other side of the ocean, so there was no need for me to feel anguished by America in regards with that either. In my reading, Russian authors always predominated, sometimes they were crowded out by Latin-Americans or the French, but even when Thornton Wilder inserted himself into this company of favorites, I didn't take him for an envoy of the United States (maybe because I had started reading him from *The Bridges of San Luis Rey* and therefore had unthinkingly assigned him at first to the Latin-American department). When I was about fifteen, a blind photocopy of Brodsky's *Parts of Speech* fell into my hands, and for many years to follow would become my poetic Bible—but here, too, America was pushed out onto the periphery of my perception by Venice and Paris. Only Ray Bradbury's *Dandelion Wine* brought America a little bit closer to my heart, because in that country, it turned out, it was possible to get ice cream at the drugstore—and not just any kind, mind you, but a lemon-and-vanilla one. It was more or less the same story with cinematography: my personal Pantheon, where Fellini, Wenders and Jarman had long ruled, Araki with *Living End,* Van Sant with *My Own Private Idaho* and Kusturica with

*Arizona Dream* entered too late—so the addition of American impressions to a European foundation never felt significant to me.

Individual incidents in my life did connect me with America from time to time, but never too seriously, not to the depths of my soul. At the high point of the bombing in Yugoslavia, when the Russian press worked itself into a lather defending the Serbian co-religionists and multi-polar world, I wrote an open letter, the idea of which was more or less that one might not necessarily approve of the bombing, but the attempts by the Russian government to gain some cheap political capital from this situation, finally joining its own people in an outpouring of anti-American hysteria, were disgusting; this letter was signed by some twenty Russian writers and was published several times—but for me it just seemed like a purely rational gesture. Another time I was invited to Iowa for three months—I don't remember exactly, some local university had a program that brought together young poets from around the world; I was asked to the embassy for an interview, I was very polite, and then they didn't even tell me I'd been rejected; after about half a year, out of pure curiosity, I asked a literary lady of my acquaintance to inquire discreetly of the cultural attaché as to why I hadn't been accepted—and it turned out, in this lady's words, to be a rather astonishing reason: everything was fine with me, in the attaché's opinion, even my lousy conversational English didn't bother him—"It's just that, you see, that Kuzmin of yours, he was much too arrogant." I laughed about that for a long time—I wasn't even offended: it's not like I was all that eager to go to Iowa. A third time—there was a documentary filmmaker from Los Angeles, shooting some footage about Russian gays, and after interviewing me he dragged me out to one of the most senselessly expensive and idiotically pretentious cafés in Moscow called, of course, "Pushkin." Fourth time . . . Fifth . . .

And yet, my staunchly aloof attitude toward America did change with time. The turning point, I believe, was poetry. It was a difficult time for me: my first poetic experiences, derived from Brodsky and authors close to him, had ceased to satisfy me: on the surface, everything seemed fine, yet something just wasn't right, the poems failed to convey the true state of my being, I looked at a sheet of paper with my poem on it and saw that it was only words, just words and nothing but—not too badly organized, perhaps, but having nothing to do with me. I stopped writing altogether and devoted myself entirely to other literary work: criticism, philology, book publishing, organizing poetry festivals; this work was far more successful and fulfilling (because good poets in Russia were quite plentiful in the mid-1990s, while good managers of the literary process could be counted on the fingers of one hand)—and frankly, I already started thinking that the young poet Dmitry Kuzmin, rather promising at one time, had died a natural death. But one day the Petersburg poet, writer, and translator Vassily Kondratiev—later he would fall to his death from a rooftop while trying to show some friends where my great predecessor and namesake, the Russian poet Mikhail Kuzmin, had lived—Vasya Kondratiev, in connection with one of my philological inquiries, gave me a thick volume of poetry written by an American I had not heard of before. This was Charles Reznikoff.

I have translated more than seventy of Reznikoff's poems over the years, enough for a good-sized book (maybe someday I'll get around to publishing them). And with this work, I think, came a new understanding: this, I realized, is what I would like to say in my own voice. Both Reznikoff's texts and his biography make it quite clear that he was someone not at all like me—yet there's a certain paradigm in his poetry which happens to coincide with what I'd been searching for in vain for the purposes of my own writing: a dry, dispassionate chronicle (what Brodsky only declares in one line: "A list of some observations"), arranged in such a way as to serve at the same time as a stenogram of heart's movements. Of course, in Russian poetry this method had also been tried out (half a century before Reznikoff), but it was Reznikoff (strangely enough, neither the Imagists nor the Objectivists ever became quite so close to me) who pushed me over to the side where, it seems, I was able to find myself—my own intonational nuance and point of view, which does not disappear from the poem once I've finished and looked over it for the first time, and that allows me, at the very least, not to feel like a hypocrite when I occasionally (as rarely as possible, but all the same) say of myself: "I am a poet." And the fact that, in addition to everything else, Reznikoff was a very *American* poet, deeply rooted in his country's history, firmly attached to the concrete features of its geography—for the first time began to warm me up to America.

The second shift in my perception of America occurred in 1998. I was turning thirty—a good reason to become depressed, start contemplating the fact that your youth has finally passed and neither dancing until dawn to trance and ambient music nor buying yourself a pair of shoes from "Swear" (red-violet with silver stripes, on ten-centimeter platforms) would mitigate that circumstance. While in this frame of mind, I received, upon returning home one morning, an unexpected happy-birthday via e-mail. My former classmate had written to me from Boston—my first love from high-school days. I didn't know that he was in Boston—a few years earlier I ran into my old girlfriend from those same times, with a charming baby by her fourth husband in tow, and from what she told me then I gathered that Pashka had gone to Australia.

He had not wished me happy birthday once since our high-school graduation—never wished me one at all, come to think of it: we hung out with different crowds and became close (albeit not as close as I'd dreamed of being) for a very short time only. Even at sixteen, I had willfulness to spare: I knew that he felt nothing for me, but I still wanted to become indispensable to him. This I managed to accomplish in half a year—the last half-year of our joint high-school past; and as a result, when the time came for him to take university entrance exams, Pashka asked me to accompany him to the first one and meet him afterward—with me around he wasn't quite so scared. The exams, needless to say, were failed, Pashka was drafted into the army, and everything ended: returning to Moscow after two years, he avoided meeting me, and when we ran into each other in the subway, he wouldn't look at me (apparently, during those two years he spent in the army, they managed to explain to him how a real man should behave toward a fag who's in love with him).

And now, in Boston, he feels rotten to the point of remembering someone who loved him on the other side of the globe, an eternity ago. Finds my

CV through Yahoo or AltaVista, notes my date of birth, waits for that date (a week? a month? half a year?), so as not to write just out of the blue, but with a reason. Finds no topic for writing, rambles on, complaining about his thinning hair (and this—straight from Brodsky again: "here I'll live out my days, losing/hair, teeth, verbs, suffixes . . ."—I doubt Pashka had ever read him), his dreary job as a computer programmer in an investment firm, about American girls, who are stupid and have huge butts, nothing like girls back in Russia . . .

I answered him as calmly as I could. Not a word about my heart, still skipping a beat at the memories of his rolling, burring r's, his fluffy white wool sweater, the fleeting smile with which he would listen to the plainest of Beatles tunes. Only one phrase—about the red dwarf rabbit living with us, named in his honor. Our correspondence failed to take hold: I probably did scare him off, after all, with that rabbit story—and what would we correspond about, anyway? But now, as a result, America became for me not just the country where in 1918 the young Charles Reznikoff published his first collection of poems on a printing press in his parents' basement—but also the country where my first love drinks vodka like there's no tomorrow, dislikes himself in the mirror, pines for Russian girls, and sometimes thinks of me . . .

And then came September 2001. The events of September 11 found me in the jam-packed basement of one of Moscow's major literary clubs: it was a reading to mark the publication of an annual anthology of young writers—a few minutes before it started, my friend the poet Lvovsky managed to tell me, "Both towers collapsed, the third plane the Americans brought down themselves"; I opened the evening, and the very first reader, Galya Zelenina, a frail girl in a little jacket, author of the best lesbian lyric poetry in Russia today, instead of reading called for a moment of silence.

Standing silent under the low, smoky arches of the club, looking at a room full of confused young faces, some of which belonged to the near future of Russian poetry at its best, I thought for a moment that perhaps it might be better to cancel the whole thing. But on the other hand, poetry (if it's real) is one of the highest manifestations of the Western intellectual tradition's concept of the uniqueness of the individual. The poet is only worth something when he is irreplaceable, when no one else can say what he can, and in the way that he can. Contemporary Western society, cut to MacLuhan's specifications, is none too hot a hothouse for unique person-alities, but neither history nor contemporary reality can offer us any more attractive variants: all the available alternatives (including the one that animated the Sept. 11 plotters) in one way or another deny individuals the right to choose, the right to their own voices. And if this is so, then at a time when this society, along with the intellectual tradition it represents, has been dealt such a horrific blow, the poet must speak, not stay silent. Even if only to speak about some other topic.

And two months later, in another Moscow literary club, Kirill Medvedev, one of the most talented poets of the younger generation, as well as a Charles Bukowski translator, read his new major work, entitled, quite straightforwardly, "Text Dedicated to the Events of September 11 in New York." The text was very powerful, its basic subject matter recalled the profound confusion of a young intellectual (it would be better to say— *intelligent,* because it is precisely the Russian *intelligentsia* that this state of profound confusion behooves the most) caused by the September trag-edy. Breaking through the chaos of contradictory, mutually antagonistic thoughts and emotions, time and again this notion sounded in Medvedev's hero's mind: "America fucked up with her political correctness. America fucked up with her humanism." And it was then that I suddenly realized: for the first time in my life, I felt something akin to solidarity with that superpower across the ocean, which I had never visited and not in the least longed for. Don't get me wrong: it's not as if I on some rational level ap-prove of, for example, U.S. policy in Afghanistan—I doubt that I have a sufficient grasp of the problem to be able to judge this policy. No; I'm just trying on, if you will, a certain set of circumstances—and I understand that if some miserable, wretched dimwit, tanked up on vodka, breaks the glass in the entryway of my apartment building, takes a whiz in the el-evator, curses after me in foul language because I have more money than he does and because I live, breathe, love, not in a way that he can comprehend; if, in the end, this dimwit gets bold and punches me in the face or demands my wallet—then however many perfectly correct arguments I could have with myself about the fact that he had a difficult childhood and a bad upbringing, or that he has an elderly mother and a young sister, both of whom adore him, even though he's ruining their lives with his drunken debauchery, or that he even has his own inner world of sorts and his own intrinsic worth—still, my only true desire consists of bashing his head against a wall until he's half-dead. Because it's too late to reeducate him, while teach him a lesson one must.

That evening, to put it simply, for one minute I felt myself to be the United States of America. And since then, I can no longer say that I am completely indifferent to that country. Although if somehow I ever get a week or two of spare time—I dream of visiting Denmark. Luxembourg I've already seen, and it's wonderful.

*Translated by Dawn L. Hannaham*

# When I Think of America . . .

## Aleksandr Levin

When I think of America, I think of how I have never been there.

At that I think right away of the man who denied my wife and me our tourist visas, the man who wanted none of my explanations, but who announced instead that the rejection was final. I try to recall, but cannot remember, his face. I recall the humiliating procedure of getting rejected. I remember I had to pay twice to get the rejection, $90 each time, and I am repulsed by my own stupidity like a jerk who remembers how he has been had before by the same pickpocket in front of the same bank exchange window.

The first half of my life was spent learning to live as though the Soviet mechanism that surrounded me was not there, as though that whole lifeless depressing monolith was not hanging over me. And having eventually learned, and even gotten used to, this state of freedom—internal at first, and then external as well, starting in the early '90s—I was forced unexpectedly to live again through the whole range of Soviet emotions. For some reason they seemed especially painful to me now. I believe it's because my immune system had weakened, my skin grown thin—I'd forgotten how it feels to deal with superiors. Because I have long ceased to have superiors. Because I have grown accustomed to considering myself a human being.

Thanks to the American youth who refreshed my memory, bringing back the warm recollections of the Soviet bureaucratic machine. Before it I was always in debt, always somehow at fault, often without knowing for what exactly. The machine that could not and would not consider my circumstance. Thanks for letting me know that the world is the same through and through. That to the U.S. government I am also already indebted and somehow have already blundered before it.

I am sad I did not get to go to America, to visit with college friends, to read them my new poems and sing them new songs. (The man at the

American Embassy could tell right away I was trying to fool him when I was unable to tell him through which immigration program the friend I'd be staying with had arrived in the U.S. some ten years prior—as though that is the only thing Russians could talk about!)

Sad to have missed New York's museums—after Parisian, Roman and Florentine ones, I had wanted to go there especially.

Sad that I could not drive across all of America with my friend, who had planned to take me on my own road movie.

Sad especially that I don't know precisely what else I don't know about America.

"Nothing personal," my friends say. Stupid to jump to conclusions based on one random fact, I am told by my common sense. And I try not to jump to conclusions.

Yet I am a poet and used to approaching the world in specifics, not generally. "Generally" I know a lot of different things about America (for instance, that America is a country in which wild bears walk down the streets pillaging garbage cans). But this is my only private impression.

Actually, when I think of America, I think how if I had gotten to see it I would think of it differently.

*Translated by Katya Kumkova-Wolpert*

# The Zoo of Freedom and the Russian Mentality

### Sergey Leybgrad

*I'll measure Manhattan north-to-south and back*
*Where the moon hangs above a cement-laden sack,*
*A signaling droplet, alive*
*Joins minute to minute, and suture by stitch*
*A mazurka assembled by night's murky pitch.*

This poem by the Russian émigré poet Aleksey Tsvetkov rang steadily in my head from the minute our Boeing landed at Kennedy airport to the moment when the real, unimagined New York appeared in my line of sight. New York with its age-old, fantastically strong metal fire grids. New York with the "small," Theodore Dreiser-era skyscrapers, maddening in their sturdiness. New York with the ruthlessly masterful 100-floor buildings, at whose foundations taxi cabs crowded together, genteel homeless New Yorkers dozed off peacefully, and among them paraded unhurriedly . . . yes, yes, it was worth looking closer . . . squirrels.

The Second Worldwide Congress of the Russian-Language Press. This was the strange and somewhat bombastic title of the event that was my reason for visiting America in the spring of 2000. For seven days—six at New York's Sheraton hotel and a day in Washington—Russian-speaking and Russian-writing citizens from more than thirty countries assembled at the cusp of April and May, looking as though they were there to discuss the real importance and true culturally-political meaning of some major historical cusp. "New President, New Russia: Metropolis and Diaspora," thus stood the exhausting wording of the congress's subject. And yet somehow we managed not to exhaust the topic, and, to be honest, we did not really try.

The mood of the conference was set by representatives of the big-city media and by the journalists from the oldest émigré newspaper *Novoye Russkoye Slovo*. In those days it was about to hit ninety years old. If you ask me, the session devoted to this anniversary was the juiciest part of the congress. Of course, in terms of official legitimacy brought to the forum it could not compare to the speeches of Mikhail Gorbachev and foreign minister Igor Ivanov—these, as they say, were the "presentable episodes." But Mikhail Sergeyevich was as culturally uncouth and verbose as ever, and Igor Ivanov—forcibly diplomatic and dutifully well-wishing. The anniversary of the *Novoye Russkoye Slovo* attracted quite a variety of names and faces. Sculptor Ernst Neizvestniy, essayist Aleksandr Genis, artist Mikhail Shemyakin, cellist Mstislav Rastropovich, writer Vassily Aksyonov, critic Svyatoslav Belza, Bel Kaufman, author of *Up the Down Staircase* and a granddaughter of Sholem Aleykhem . . .

Still—why hide this?—my favorite, my most passionate and most wonderful conversation partner, the Event, in the grand and the small senses, proved to be not the terrific forum itself, but, first and foremost, his un-regal majesty New York. Yes, there was also DC, with its marble quasi-Roman architecture: the White House and Capitol building, which we visited alongside a delegation from some American province (what a sight it is, damn it, watching full-bodied school girls, in sundresses, all blissful smiles, observing the stuffy old congressmen in their session); the mile-long stretch of free museums (thank you for Rauschenberg, Warhol, Kandinsky and Jones . . .).

And yet it's precisely the singing, dancing, chewing, restless and sleepless New York, on its tippy toes, always reaching up high with its skyscrapers, that dealt the most devastating yet most tender blow to my heart. Shimmer and garbage, the homeless and squirrels, jazz and the classics, grand museums and hundreds of galleries, the Metropolitan and the constructivist Guggenheim, Chinatown and Little Italy, comical Brighton Beach and the kindly Babylonian Broadway . . .

I am almost offended that New York for its part did nothing to impress us. It was obnoxious, elegant and carefree, unbelievably clean and equally dirty, clever and vulgar, aristocratic and crass.

"Skyscrapers, skyscrapers, and I'm so, so small . . ." What nonsense, really, this Willy Tokarev[1] song is. The sense of mythology, a feeling of

---

[1]  A Russian-emigre performer popular in Brighton Beach, the largely Russian community in Brooklyn.

my own giganticness—this is what filled my longing, cowardly, wounded heart. I was stopped nowhere and by no one. I did not speak to anyone, but everyone spoke to me. Seeing my saddened face cab drivers stopped to sing me a song, squirrels from Central Park threw themselves at my feet, and policemen of all colors nodded at me with sympathy. Poets and merchants, musicians and clerks, fatsoes and pigmies, Chinese and blacks, Jews and gentiles, Indians and Hindus were in delirium, sick with that famous, generalized yet deeply personal, American freedom. "I love," maintained the billboards, tents, T-shirts and plastic bags; repeated official signs; and spelled out the letters on flags and cars. The city of blooming Japanese cherry trees and tulips from Holland, the city of immigrants . . .

I will never live in New York. The very thought that someone will give me—a hand-me-down—freedom, dignity and a real chance at happiness is the thought of a slave. An uncultured thought. I will never—never ever—live in New York.

It seems that it's not just us, but the whole civilized world that can't comprehend what, after all, happened—Bin Laden and all . . . After the tragedy in New York the twenty-first century might have arrived. Of its own accord. Without our input. Terrorists, of course, are just that—terrorists. But I think September 11 was a vision dreamed up not only by the maddest of movie directors, but by all of us who had quietly envied America its American dream and American dignity, which to justify ourselves we called "obnoxious," or "individualistic," or simply "barbaric" . . .

I don't love anyone on this earth, how do I stop loving you? It's hard to call things and events by their real names. Even when you're alone. Especially when these things and events don't have names yet. When they no longer have names . . .

In the distance, under a sleeping sun, the Statue of Liberty stubbornly keeps on holding a torch in her hand, which is stretched out to the sky. At every stand, in every small shop, thousands, hundreds of thousands, of small, inexplicably green Statues of Liberty . . . But there is no liberty in your head, your heart, your memory, your movements, your gaze . . .

I love no one on earth . . . No, I do love. I love New York City, which I visited in the spring of 2000. Samara doesn't count. There's no way I can get rid of Samara, with all my childhood scars, fears and hopes. Samara does not count. I remember how at The Eaglet youth summer camp,[2] as the sun set one night, I explained to a black American boy that I come from the city of Kuybyshev, which is really called Samara. It was our first night at The Eaglet. Michael, who was of basketball height, took me for a girl named Tamara from Kuybyshev on the Volga. Imagine his surprise when we ran into each other again in the men's room, a half hour later. For the rest of the session, smiling his broad kind smile, he called me Tamara . . . Later, on the soccer field, I showed him which one of us was the real *girl*. That day we bombed the world youth league team, and after the game, raising his thumb in the air, he told me that from now on he would call me simply "Samara" . . .

Lyudmila Putina (President Putin's wife) recently visited The Eaglet. She pronounced some words appropriate for the occasion, admitting that she envied today's children. She sang a few pioneers' songs, hugging the kids by their shoulders. Oh, how I used to hate those false, artificial songs. The whole lot of the sexually obsessed pioneer scout leaders and Komsomol members, who sang of young eaglets and blue nights in the daytime, and cursed and moaned at night in drunken copulation. Things you should always do joyously, purely, charmingly and organically they managed to make dirty, feverish, low . . .

Now their children have joined the "Walking Together"[3] movement. They are afraid of their freedom and their own bodies. Instead of loving, they are dirty, feverish, low. For this they take their revenge on uncensored writers. Or rather, through them those pioneer scout leaders and Komsomol members of my very youth are able to have their revenge . . .

I love New York City. Though that city probably doesn't exist any-

---

[2]  A prestigious summer camp for the politically active youth in the Crimea.

[3]  A political movement of patriotically minded youths supportive of president Putin and organized around charges of obscenity against the work of some Russian novelists, such as Vladimir Sorokin and Viktor Pelevin.

more . . . Definitely, it does not exist. Those funny, singing, chewing, reading people . . . Those funny old ladies in Central Park, walking a whole litter of spoiled pups in their lacy outfits. The hairy painters on every corner . . . The old, pension-aged rockers, belting John Lennon songs on the lawn in front of the park, a choir of Japanese boys singing Mozart nearby . . . I don't know why, but I nearly started to cry when a red-haired girl, about fourteen, charming and plump like Lolita, pressed herself to me in fright. Somehow we ended up next to each other in a tight ring of people. We sat on the stairs, again in Central Park, while in front of us a group of black boys beat out a juicy rhythm on plastic buckets and spun unbelievable somersaults with no one to spot them. At the end, the smallest performer was launched high into the sky and, having flipped over thrice in the air, he landed softly on his feet and began to spin elegant breakdancing shapes on the ground. Making sure that the young acrobat was alive and well, my Lolita pulled away and, without so much as a look back at me, got up to thank the wandering artists. The audience, childishly stupid looks on their faces, threw coins, sang along and read out some kind of rhymes. Frightened, cowardly, greedy and insecure, I wiped the idiotic tears of happiness from my ever-sad face. For a few minutes I forgot about my fears, my debts and my cares, about lowly thoughts and shameful desires . . . I spent the whole day wandering Manhattan, and all day I wanted someone to stop me. I had no weapons or drugs, and the devices fashioned at exits and entrances did not react to me. Not once did anyone stop me. I was free and of no use to anyone. Doubtful of my own existence I froze at a street corner, aware of the piercing gaze of a driver, which was focused upon me. Deliberately his Jeep did not move. A row of cars stretched out behind him, some of them honking maniacally without end. My driver kept looking at me, smiling and singing loudly, showing the "fuck you" sign to the impatient motorists. Finally, I understood what he wanted: for me to trade in the tragic Pierrot mask for a reciprocal smile. I smiled, he was off . . .

I love that New York which probably doesn't exist anymore. The city of writers, artists and professorish-looking homeless men, the city of books and museums, cheap souvenirs and thick daily papers. The city of multi-colored immigrants who have forgotten they're orphans. The city that now again lives its own life, a life separate from mine.

And here in Samara, at the edges of silence, it's feminine rhymes, raw nerve endings. It's hard to call things and events by their real names. Even when you're alone. Especially when these things and events don't yet have names . . .

*Translated by Katya Kumkova-Wolpert*

# Forever and the Earth[1]

## Stanislav Lvovsky

The author's birthday falls on July 2. His twenty-six-year-old mother couldn't hold on until Independence Day. And so. The summer of 1972 was hot, the peat bogs around Moscow burned, just as they did in 2002.

Just before I arrived in this world, Nixon came to Moscow and they signed a treaty to limit strategic weapons. It seems to have given up the ghost for good not long ago, that treaty. Later, already with me being extant, this Nixon (for some reason I always felt sorry for him) will get himself enmeshed in an unpleasant story with listening devices in a hotel with a famous name—does this hotel still exist, and how do its current guests feel?

They kept bombing North Vietnam until the 30th of December, but it was already clear that things would end as we now know they did. In 1973, Brezhnev said that the Cold War had ended. But it would not end anytime soon—this my parents still did not know then, but they would find out later. Because my father was left without a job after Reykjavik[2]—the outfit he worked for made radio-location stations, whose task it was to keep us informed in the event of the American missiles' launch from their bases in Western Europe (flight time: seven minutes, if anyone remembers).

I celebrated Independence Day in Moscow, the summer of 1996, if memory serves me. The woman with whom I lived at the time, and whom I loved beyond all reason, worked in the Moscow office of Bristol Myers-Squiggs, which supplied our country with aspirin and other useful substances; and she received an invitation for two people—American employees only, the holiday was domestic in nature, generally speaking; the American Chamber of Commerce rented the Kuskovo Park—a clear summer night with the firework display was over the pond, Marines at

---

[1]   Title of a Ray Bradbury novel.

[2]   Site of the Reagan-Gorbachev summit in 1985.

the gates, and *From sea to shining sea* to wrap things up in the end. One of my most vivid memories on the subject of emotional commonality; I realized then that all these people really did feel themselves to be one nation and really loved their country—in a perfectly, it seemed, romantic way.

My biography as a reader was formed in a completely atypical fashion. My father, despite his aggressive occupation, was an Americanophile through and through—and doubtless an internal émigré—and our house was filled with American literature, both contemporary and not quite, which Soviet publishers brought out in great quantities at the time. Thus it came about that it was Thomas Wolfe, Sherwood Anderson, Salinger, Flannery O'Connor, Vonnegut, Faulkner and Bradbury I most likely got around to reading before familiarizing myself, at some point in eighth grade, with Tolstoy, Dostoyevsky, and Turgenev. I am afraid I owe less to Rudin and Ivanov and Sonechka Marmeladova than to George Webber,[3] the Glass family and the inhabitants of Yoknapatawpha County. As I clambered up to the bookcase's top shelf, in order to take out the next *Intruder in the Dust,* a smiling, white-toothed Ella Fitzgerald followed me with her eyes. And in my high-school graduation essay I wrote on *Catcher in the Rye*—the tenor of the times had already changed by then, had become sufficiently, in Akhmatova's expression, "vegetarian."

With music, it was a whole separate story—starting with just that very Ella's Amiga[4] record—concert in Berlin, the black spiral circling narrowly to the center, "How High the Moon" and "Mack the Knife"—and everything else, including Armstrong, came later. To this day, despite not having listened to jazz for a long time (not enough of a *draiv* in it, for today's me), every so often I still play that record, remembering how the sheer essence of my being (where'd it disappear since?) used to flutter against my diaphragm at its opening drumbeats.

When I was a little older, there came movies—Sam Peckinpah's *Convoy* (God only knows how it managed to make it onto Soviet silver screens)

---

[3]   Hero of Thomas Wolfe's *You Can't Go Home Again.*

[4]   State-owned recording firm in the former German Democratic Republic.

and *The Day After* (no such mystery in *its* case)—from which it became clear as day even to the schoolboy that I was that the Americans were no less scared of us than we were of them. I remember vividly how as a child I used to have nightmares about the bomb falling directly underneath our window—we lived on the first floor of a large apartment building. I will never forget how my uncle, an architect, man of perfectly peaceable pursuits, made a mad dash to the portable radio at his *dacha:* he thought he'd heard an air-raid warning siren. I looked at his trembling hands (he just couldn't catch "Mayak," the mainstay of state radio stations). I was dead for those seven minutes. And the heady feeling of incredible recognition— many years later, on the last sentence of Charles Bukowski's story "Animal Crackers in my Soup": "The nurse stood holding my child in her hands as the first hydrogen bomb fell on San Francisco."

As you can tell from this erratic narrative, all of my experiences related to America have been of a derivative character. Text, music, films, photos—Joan Baez, entering the Berkeley campus with a guitar at the ready, articles about Jerry Rubin circulating in blind photocopies, *Where have you been, my blue-eyed son,* and Soviet hippies circa the end of the 1980s, born wholly out of some vague longing for a different, foreign kind of life—one which *over there,* far away, had long since ceased to exist, while *over here* it had never begun in the first place. And so it remains derivative, vicarious, this American experience of mine: nothing but words, tiny little symbols.

At the end of the 1990s, after I broke up with the woman who worked at BMS, I had a long and perfectly strange virtual romance with an American girl from California. The mother of charming twins, a housewife, she apparently felt a lack of excitement in her life and made up for it in the safest way she could think of (conservative family back in Alabama, family values, always vote Republican, you get the picture). The impossibility of our ever meeting in real life lent a bitter aftertaste to our romance, and supplied the emotional heat that would hardly have been possible under more normal circumstances. Thus I learned how to write about love in English. *Natasha, Natasha, how are Benjamin and Jonathan, we haven't written to each other in two years already,* I'm beginning to forget all these *tender words, nezhniye slova,* ah well, it's not that important, after all. I told you already—words, nothing but tiny little symbols, the flimsy fabric of two mutually incompatible languages falling apart in our hands.

In 1994 I graduated from the chemistry department at Moscow State University. Everything was still ahead of me—that Independence Day of 1996, and the first letter from Natasha, and even the Bukowski stories I had not yet read, to say nothing of the poems of his I would later be translating (still do, sometimes), feeling somehow a keen affinity with that graphomaniac-alcoholic, who spent his whole life, it seems, without ever getting out from behind the typewriter—well, judging, at least, by the sheer volume of his output. Within a year and a half after graduation, I already lost the majority (if not all) of my close friends, as they left to study science in the States—because to study science in today's Russia means to doom oneself to a life of wretched misery.

Then again, not everyone was quite so devoted to science. A., for one, just didn't want to breathe this air and perform in theaters here, keep climbing their endless career ladders, on whose every landing one had to screw yet another director or stagehand. L. and V. were tired of living in the Kuzminki *micro-district* of Moscow, populated predominantly by illegal immigrants (poor economical situation, high crime rate)—well, I apologize: those two, they are in Canada—but do you really think the difference is all that noticeable from down here? E. was simply born for the USA—and indeed, he now works as a business consultant for AT&T—here there was just not enough room for him, and the rules of the game were too, how should I put it, too *fluid,* and this latter circumstance outweighed in the end all the infinitely more promising career possibilities open to a manager here in Russia.

They all long ago got married, had families, developed a clear idea of where they'd like to see themselves in the future—which is something that's impossible here, where we live on ice that could start to crack beneath our feet at any moment. I'm already thirty and, God knows, it's already been seven years—yet to this day I continue to feel this exodus (of our class of 150, only ninety still remain in Russia) as a personal loss of something entirely irretrievable. No, there is no more emigration; it was in the old days, in *Bolshevik* times, that those who were about to leave became as good as dead to those who stayed behind, that farewells were tantamount to funerals because those staying behind knew with utmost certainty that they'd never again see those who were leaving. It's all different now—to travel is too far, too expensive, there's no time to call, and it's not a dark-watered river but the Atlantic Ocean that separates here and there, just an eight-hour flight, but then one's whole night passes in eight hours. And it's even longer to get to the West Coast. Eleven hours' difference.

Going back, rewinding the thick tape in the unwieldy *magnitofon* of my childhood. Latvia—still, back then, the westernmost edge of the Soviet empire, a small house almost at the seashore—and, through the howling of jamming installations: "This is the Voice of America"; they (you) were reading to us Vassily Aksyonov's *The Island of the Crimea,* a novel the existence of which no one except those of us who heard him read from it then ever suspected at the time (nor do they now, I'm afraid). "Liberty Live" on your airwave, *Svoboda v pryamom efire,* and I, a ten-year-old boy, I listen to these voices, as they break through the jamming, and I almost faint from the feeling, the sense that right here, very close by, there is another, a whole other world, unattainable, foreign, impossible, wonderful, unattainable, foreign.

I foreswore myself from writing about how much I hate the U.S. Embassy (please provide the documentation of your claim that you own purebred dogs in Russia, in support of your stated intention to return), which has done away with the presumption of innocence, forcing *me* to prove that I do not intend to remain in the United States. I do not. If there ever was something that I wanted to write about, it would only be about love, longing, separation, about *a stone, a leaf, an unfound door, a lost, and by the wind grieved, ghost* (Thomas Wolfe), that today is *a perfect day for bananafish,* and "pozhaluista, priezzhai v Boston," please come to Boston, and *New York says to Moscow: Moscow, Moscow, take me with you,* so it goes, *not a word about love and death,* just as I promised. And one more thing I want to tell you:

I have never been to America, these are all just tiny little symbols, a mere word, impossible to translate into English, the Amiga record, Watergate, the portrait of Ella, @unr.edu, end of December, four A.M., Leonard Cohen's song (do you really think there's any difference when looking from here?), *where is my see more glass* (Salinger), straw dogs (Pekinpah), Mulder and Scully, *bukovki,* Russia, America, cold war, hot milk.

I would like to end with a quote, one of those remembered since childhood. For example: "Seymour once said that all we do all our lives is go from one piece of Holy Ground to the next. Is he *never* wrong?" (*Franny and Zooey*)

Never. Never.

*Translated by Dawn L. Hannaham*

# Worn Jeans and Banned Fruits

## Aleksey Mikheev

My first retained impression of America was the film *It's a Mad, Mad, Mad, Mad World* (Kubrick? Kramer?) in the panoramic Mir theater on Tsvetnoi Boulevard in Moscow around '64. The theater was, like the film, also quite mad, with its gigantic, wide-frame screen, reaching up to the very ceiling. I, at eleven years of age, sat in a first row seat on the side and, leaning my head back and to the left, watched with an open mouth as fantastic, handsome automobiles furiously chased and collided with one another on the screen: not our banal Volgas and Moskviches, but genuine Fords, Chryslers, and Cadillacs.

Then came the end of the sixties (hippies, Woodstock)—and the image of America as a romantic land of boundless freedom, where thanks to the *easy riders* the *Flower Power* finally prevailed. It's true, Hendrix, Joplin, and Morrison departed shortly thereafter to the other world, but Lennon still remained. The fact that he, of all people, America didn't accept (having killed him in the end) seemed insignificant at the time. Our euphoria from the idealistic notion of this cross-oceanic paradise on the other side of the iron curtain was stronger than any uncomfortable facts. And the first ones to leave for America departed as lucky men, delivered forever from melancholy, dejection, and oppression.

In the beginning of the eighties, hopelessly trapped in the "Evil Empire," it was only fitting to gaze upon America as our only ray of hope. All the more so because, as Radio Liberty was being jammed like there was no tomorrow, the Voice of America's broadcasts from Washington were quite accessible, even if only in English, and it was possible to catch the news about Babrak Karmal in Kabul, Walesa and Yaruzelski in Warsaw, and Sakharov in Gorky. But then in the end of the eighties, when Gorbachev got out of his car on a New York street to shake hands with common passersby, there was a fresh emergence of euphoria. It became even stronger when Yeltsin appeared before the U.S. Congress: after his statement about the final collapse of communism in Russia, our president received a standing ovation. It soon came to pass that many more handsome automobiles began to appear in Russia and coupons for vodka were finally abolished (which had seemed extremely unlikely at one time, but then turned out to be true), and that Russians and Americans again, like they had been on the banks of Elba, would be brothers forever (which seemed more likely, but never did come true in the end).

Then the hangover rolled in. America suddenly materialized in the guise of McDonald's, McDucks, Madonnas and Michael Jacksons. It was as though your youthful bride, from whom you were separated for twenty years, finally showed up in your home—vulgar, loud, flabby, with dyed hair and gum in her mouth: *"Hey, boy, you were so lonesome* without me, but everything's behind us, now we will be *happy together forever."* Like when Mordyukova[1] pressed poor Vitsin,[2] in that old movie *The Marriage of Balzaminov,* against a fence: "Come to me . . . you . . . I want you . . . ev-very day . . ." I watched the first *Star Wars* in 1979 with much bewilderment: could they be taking this kindergarten stuff seriously? Quite seriously, it turned out—along with Batman, Godzilla, aliens and blazing skyscrapers.

In 2001, when skyscrapers blazed in flames not on the movie screen but in reality, sympathy was, alas, less prominent than fear in Russia. People had already had plenty of time to get used to catastrophe and violent death on the tube (thanks, incidentally, to Hollywood and CNN, in large measure). Several thousand dead people didn't really count, especially since they were dead several thousand kilometers away. As for fear, the inevitable American retaliatory strike against the whole infamous "axis of evil"—what if the Godzilla paw of American military might, in its blind rage, were to slam down on us too, by pure accident? There might not be an escape from America in search of a scapegoat! And one other fear was born, albeit one of lesser significance: what if tomorrow those little green

---

[1] A popular Russian film actress.

[2] A popular Russian comic film actor.

pieces of papers with portraits of dead presidents on them were to become useless all of a sudden, drastically devalued overnight, and along with the World Trade Center, the last pillars of financial stability in the world would collapse?

(A digression. This past summer I happened to pass through Belgrade. Some of the ruins left after the American bombing raids still haven't been cleared out—people are afraid there could be unexploded bombs inside there. But something else struck me as quite amazing: several McDonald's on neighboring streets were open and seemed to be doing just fine. Not one of their windows had been broken, even! One cannot but wonder: if NATO had bombed out the Ostankinsky TV-tower (why not, after all, given the Russian TV-coverage of the war in Chechnya!), would Muskovites remain faithful to hamburgers with cola? And those bad, evil Serbs, they just couldn't care less!)

So then, there you have it: a subjective evolution of the image of America in one's mind over the past, almost, forty years. My present attitude towards it can be expressed best by the old (mid-eighties still!) Aleksandr Butusov song: "They grew much too tight for me, your worn blue jeans / for oh so long they taught us / to love your forbidden fruits!" And, of course, the refrain: "Goodbye, America, oh, where I will never be . . ." It looks like, indeed, I never will be there. For one thing, no one's inviting me. Secondly, I already somehow got past the urge to go. And finally, it seems like life in Russia today is a whole lot more fun and interesting course than it is in America—at the very least, we don't have its paranoid political correctness and all those idiotic petty prohibitions, like the one that says you can't drink beer on the street.

*Translated by Andrea Gregovich*

# America As Freedom and Image

## Dmitry Prigov

It comes to . . . it comes back to such banal ideas and claims: anytime we're hashing it out or figuring things out with someone else, it's the same hashing and figuring out that we have going on with ourselves and our Others and our image of the other. Especially when that sort of thing happens on our own Russian turf. In other words, it's about American turf, but it's happening on Russian ideological and spiritual-mental turf. Or, say, to be contrary, on Danish turf. Where would you have me get a different one? I don't have it. And no one has it. You could, of course, decline hashing things out in favor of the no less banal description of scenes from someone else's everyday life, the shocking details and meetings with so-called interesting people. But there are interesting people everywhere. Though, of course, any old sniper or murderer in America is extraordinary, even when compared to unusual Russian cutthroats. But all that comes from the media. Where in real-life America would you find these articulators of national idiosyncrasies? While, in Russia, meeting these folks is no problem. But we're not talking about them, nor about Russia. We're concerned with the Russian reaction to America. We could, of course, talk about the simpler things that just jump straight out at you. But why? Really, why? It all comes out to the same thing. It's already started. Now it's almost out.

And, by the way, America really has a lot that's reminiscent of Russia, which eases the trauma of the first encounter. Well, first of all, they've got a lot of people who speak English (I won't say what kind), and they exchange dollars, which we're quite used to in our new Russian life. That makes it easier. Secondly, it's pleasing to notice the rising number of Russian-speaking gentlemen and comrades, and to see how they're finally coming into their own self-awareness and social self-organization, on the example set by other American ethnic communities. Perhaps something good will come of it, in the vein of lobbies for Russian interests and the ingraining of all

sorts of Russian cultural stuff with all the requisite honorariums and pop-
ularity the participants expect. And then there's the gigantic geographi-
cal stretches, the long crossings, which we somehow considered the sole
property of Russian existence, our unique national pride. At first it sur-
prises, but then consoles and even relaxes the first-time visitor. And it's
not without the contrasts so beloved of the Soviet ideological establishment and the biased view of today's Russian consumers. But they do exist.
And we're used to them ahead of time. Although you won't find anything
like Harlem even in our most self-respecting larger cities. Of course, of
course, we've got plenty of those God-forsaken places left to rot, but none
of them have the same quality or pathos of continual self-destruction that's
in Harlem and its replicas in other American megacities. Well, all right.
It's not for us to mete out judgments.

All these remarks accumulate a special meaning if one keeps in mind
that the Russian utopia of a successful world order, which tortures us and
everyone in our proximity, has long shifted from Europe to America. And
America presents enough opportunities to dig into it, and just as many reasons to discover, with sick satisfaction, that it doesn't hold up. But curiously
enough, what is constant in the centuries-long existence of this torturous and
weak Russian fascination, which has at different times been projected onto
various geographic, ethnic, political and social spaces, is the sense that *they*
lack in spirituality, in the rarified air necessary for sacred Russian breathing.
And, truly, where would *they* get it over there? Plus, of course, with the total
knowledge of how they, the ignorant, over there, should administer their
good fortune and set everything up in the best possible manner. And, in the
same way we dressed ourselves in something like Asiatic animal skins in defiance of European snobbery, so in opposition to feisty America we seem as if
to don culture-centric European tuxes. But there's something to this! No?
You don't think so? Well, fine. But still, there's something in it.

Anyhow, our complexes really are European. In the sense that we've obtained them together with Europe itself in the period after World War II.
Taking into account, of course, the whole gamut of social, cultural, and scien-
tific achievements and failures within Europe proper, and its lag from Russia.

In other words, all those gripes about various McDonald's, Burger Kings, Kentucky Fried Chickens, Michael Jacksons and Mickey Mouses (even great Russian writers, meaning women writers, meaning particularly one of them, can't help themselves from making fierce invectives against them—they're not great and Russian for nothing!). And who else? Hollywood, of course. What else? Lots, but there's no point listing all of it.

At first, upon coming to America, there's an illusion that you're speaking the same language (considering that English is rarely a problem for most of the younger population of larger Russian cities) and addressing the same problems. In fact, in the big picture of the only recent utopia to have survived—the totality of a universal anthropological foundation—that's the way it is. Everything one person might say, in principle, can be understood by another. In principle, yes. But only in the most superficial sense. And that's not taking into account that humankind is quickly moving toward a new anthropology. And that's most true in the centers of today's neo-anthropological growth and shift, the megapolises that have much more in common in any part of the world than do the countries that surround and fuel them. But this is not the place to expand on specific manifestations of the new anthropology, though they are real, unquestionable, and myriad. So back to the seeming likeness of language and subjects. To describe this situation, one metaphoric scene is quite useful. It is a made-up story which was once told to me, I think, by the artist Ilya Iosefovich Kabakov, a real master of such parables. Imagine, he said to me, you walk into a stadium and witness the one-on-one race of two long-distance runners. With all the passion and enthusiasm of a loyal fan that is intrinsic to you (though feeling the strange indifference from the rest of the stands), you plug into the battle between the athletes. And only when the runners cross the finish line do you discover that they have, by chance, coincided in space and time at the moment of your appearance in the stands. Actually, one of them has outrun the other by several laps. He has already completed the race and is already occupied with other things. And the other one has still to run and run. And perhaps he won't ever make it to the finish. That's the way it is—concluded Ilya Iosefovich. And then you find yourself lost in thought. And I was.

It should be said that in the American boondocks there's plenty of the quaint and the weird. On my first visit to America, for example, in many of the smaller towns and settlements, they know only three facts about Russia, or rather, three words and names: Sputnik, Gorbachev, and Evtushenko Babii Yar. And in the last case, they were surprised to learn from me that the phrase is made up of the poet's name and the title of his poem. I'm sure that upon my departure they again calmly forgot about it. And I'm sure that since then their information about Russia has likely not substantially increased. More likely, it's even diminished.

In Saint Louis, at my homage-exhibit to Malevich, one stylishly dressed older lady asked me: "Will the artist himself be present at the opening?" "That's me," I answered with a certain modesty. "No, the second one, will Malevich come?" "I'm not sure," I answered doubtfully.

In fact, the same abounds in other parts of the world. This isn't an exclusive American trademark. An interviewer from the cultural department of a prestigious Munich newspaper wanted to know about the Russians' knowledge of Western classics, specifically in the realm of literature and poetry. In my naiveté, I started listing some names of Western classics that had at one time or another thrilled my imagination: Villon, Goethe, Whitman, Baudelaire, Rilke, Rimbaud . . . The eyes of my interviewer reflected no acknowledgment. The list I recited elicited no reaction from her, until she suddenly latched onto the last of the names: "Really? And how did Rambo arouse your interest?" But, oh Lord, what about here at home? What about us?

I was relating to a young Moscow filmmaker, a recent graduate of VGIK,[1] the story of a discussion in a London film club after the screening of a film based on Kafka. I told him how the refined and overly intellectual president of that club, who praised the film highly and offered a meticulous critique of all its details, at the end of his talk made note of the fact that he'd never read any Kafka himself. It happens, what can you do? I was telling him all this with the goal of emphasizing the shockingly prevalent lack of culture among so-called Western intellectuals, that would be unimaginable in our own intelligentsia circles.

"Really?" replied the young Moscow filmmaker, "and who is this guy

---

[1]   The Russian State Institute of Cinematography.

Kafka?" So let us, for now, leave aside comparisons in this field.

On the whole, in principle, there's no real need to travel to America in order to know everything you need to know about it, all that's useful to know for one's own possibilities. And you might as well forget all that's impossible to find out. After all, unless you completely settle there, unless you make it your home both existentially and psychologically, it will remain a utopia, a point of extrapolative running-away in the hopes of looking back to understand one's own home. This kind of gaze is particular. This sort of looking back is amusing, shocking, and offers much to learn from. But you don't want to come out with that sudden hurt feeling and compensating snootiness which are so natural for little countries in their traumatic confrontation with the indifference of a great country, and just as natural to a provincial who looks upon the wished-for but unattainable capital. One wouldn't want to end up in the fix that I've so often noted at all kinds of meetings, conferences, discussions and symposiums, when various ambassadors of various developing countries speak their first words addressed to the confused Americans, saying: "Give us a million dollars right this second!" (or two, or three, ten, one-hundred million, depending on the ambitions and illusions of the given representative from some stepped-on country or neglected nation). And then, after quickly skipping over their speech's meaningless middle, they conclude with passion: "And go, get out of our face, let us live the way *we* think we should!" Maybe they are right. Indeed, they probably are. But one doesn't necessarily want to be likened to them. It's just tasteless, I guess.

So, in this way, it's amusing to look at America. And even more amusing—to watch her through her local tears and befuddlement.

Like the story of Monica and Bill. The interpretation on our shores saw the story as concerning the sexual virulence and masculine success of the latter. You might recall a somewhat buffoon-like participant of a similarly grotesque coup attempt. Yanaev[2] was his name. Yes, yes, I remember.

---

[2] Former vice-president in the last Soviet government and a participant of the attempted coup against Gorbachev in August of 1991.

And he's still around, I take it, but no longer in the vicious, side-taking public sphere. So it went that at the time of his installment in the seat of vice-president under Gorbachev, he answered—to a mostly male chorus of approving chuckles: "You should ask my wife. She doesn't seem to be complaining." In much the same way, I'm sure, he would have previously replied to questions about his ideological health, something like: You should ask my primary party organization.

The Clinton incident did not, as some hoped, show the world the piquant nature of those sexual relations, which were in this case nothing to write home about. Instead, it made clear to the world the status of today's politician as a pop-star, in whom the people invest so many human expectations, hopes and their own unfulfilled destinies, that he is not allowed to have any other, more private life beyond the limits of a specific image that's been forced on him. If you have been chosen as a social and moral model, then, if you please, be a darling and keep to it for the whole four years.

If Clinton had been put up as an erotic pop-figure, like Madonna, then I guess the incident would have corresponded to public expectations.

In Russia, however, and in Europe as well (especially in France and Italy) a politician remains to this day a charismatic figure free of any responsibilities toward the masses who elected him. It's more like the masses are responsible to him. That's why the career and image of a European politician are untrammeled by any political, economic, criminal or sexual scandals. They don't concern him, or else, he may even profit from them.

But the path of democracy in a society of victorious Gothams, information technology and entertainment systems—that is America's path. If, of course, one is to follow this path, one must take into account all its consequences, some of which may be totally unacceptable to people who still adhere to the formidable culture of the nineteenth century.

All told, as it is perceived by many in Russia and beyond, America has galloped off to some faraway time and space where we almost can't catch up to it (let's call this place "ahead") and, as many argue, it'll be there forever. Let us not so blindly take up solidarity with this kind of categorical thinking. Yet something of the sort does flash by in the mind of any unbiased observer. But wait, let's give it time, give it time. Even if this "forever" wavers on the horizon of historical time, still on the horizon of the average person's short human life span, it seems quite real—though it is stripped of a certain, almost metaphysical totality and masochistic pathos. Moreover, by the singular personal efforts of singular individuals, like points on a line, people can plug into this accelerating foreign way of life, and even excel in it, as exemplified by the experience of these singular individuals. But that's another story.

After all, we live in such times when the archaic idea that there is just one amazing and true thing and that everything else tries to follow its lead, with more or less success and similitude, has been many times proven wrong. The idea that one must be first, or at least in the top ten, of one's nomination, appeals to us more greatly. But what we are nominated for—to discern *that* is already a great lifetime achievement.

The situation, then, of being in the middle, the eternal race to catch up and the flinching on all sides (but certainly at a passing level of development) gives birth to quite entertaining socio-cultural monsters and centaurs, which—incidentally—don't look half bad in art.

So, let's start making art?

*Translated by Matvei Yankelevich*

# America As It Is and Is Not

## Igor Shevelev

My perception of America can best be described in words uttered by the Academician Sakharov, when he first arrived in the United States. He was riding in a luxurious car and his companions were cajoling him to look out of the window—to see how beautiful it was. He cast a brief glance—to quiet them—and said, "Yes, I have expected something like this." And then he went back to his thoughts on the issue he was discussing.

After the fall of the "Iron Curtain" the outside world lost all its charm for me and probably for a certain number of other Russian people. From now on there was nowhere to run, except inside oneself.

During Soviet times, when I found myself totally incompatible with the people around me, I felt like a Westerner, just misplaced. I am an individualist, count only on myself and my own creative potential. I could not care less about everybody else. I am a conscious opponent of collectivism in principle. It is impossible for me to say "we" in regards to somebody else. Functionaries of any level make me sick—either with rage or with nausea. No doubt, I am a Westerner.

After I went abroad for the first (and last) time, I returned not so much a patriot (if, of course, one does not regard hatred towards Russia as gut love of it—which, in fact, it is), as a person who realized that there was nowhere to run. That all of our (my) characteristics are exclusively ours (mine) in their unique configuration. That dirty streets and shitty lobbies of apartment blocks (which drive a normal liberal like me crazy), as well as the aggressiveness of people in the streets and their extreme unwillingness to give in to any discipline and accept total mediocritization, are the other side of our (my) so-called soulfulness, without which a true Western way of life seems to me (us) absolutely unbearable.

It was a mortifying discovery, I must say. For two weeks I and young Duma representatives, businessmen, lawyers, journalists toured the most attractive spots of Europe—from Strasburg and Luxemburg to Cologne and the rest of Germany. We were fed, taken to places, and hosted, we ate in chic restaurants almost all the time, we met with the top functionaries of the European Union and discussed the issues of cultural identity with the best Western minds. I returned home in such a state that my wife asked me if I had been kept in Auschwitz the whole time.

The first thing that struck me in Europe was the choral singing of Russian songs by the most liberal and progressive young Duma representatives and businessmen. Before that experience I thought that only dumb provincial Russian "chelnoki"[1] would sing in this manner while on the autobahn. By the end of the trip, having socialized with Westerners and seen the indigenous life in its every ethnic—French, Luxemburg, German, etc.—version, I stopped thinking that way. They are different. They are impossible to live with. Boring. You cannot reach their soul, and the surface is nauseating. As a result, you had to re-invent your life—in Russia. Should I, like a worm, begin digging an underground tunnel and a bunker in mid-Russia?

And America flaked off by itself. (It takes thirteen hours to get there! Give me a break…) That's taking into consideration the fact that America is close to my heart thanks to a great number of my near and dear who live there. You read some of them, listen to others, correspond with the third group, follow the life of the fourth group while constructing in your mind a more complex and ambivalent image of America itself and of yourself in it.

No doubt, the self-content "Brothers"[2] of blockbusters who crush the alien America are disgusting. Primarily, because they disgust me here, in Russia. I know them: dumb brutes, they take their world abroad. These are people who carry their ghetto around, self-content and narrow-minded.

(That's how I felt in Luxemburg's eighteenth-century castle that belonged to the local Ministry of Foreign Affairs as I watched, in horror, my countrymen singing their songs, arms round each other's shoulders. I was

---

[1] Salesmen who commuted between Western and Russian markets re-selling goods.

[2] A reference to the thuggish heroes of the popular film *Brother 2*.

looking at them through the eyes of local waiters and I realized that we would look at Nazis in Munich beer-houses in the same way.) But that's the way all people, Americans included, behave when among their countrymen abroad. That is why I am more and more disappointed in human nature rather than people, ours or foreign. And it seems to me that this disappointment is not an American response. That nation's cheerful and hard-working way of life presupposes optimism and energy, rather than resignation. Our "America," our dream is a comfortable loony bin.[3]

Yes, culture that ennobles the essence of Homo is to my liking. However, returning in my thoughts to the everyday life of quiet Western towns, I realize that I would die of boredom there, no matter how well-mannered and smiling the people are. It is alien.

In short, America for me is one of the models of Western civilization. As such, it is much more to my liberal liking than Russia. But with my whimsical subconscious, in which emotions beat any reason, I could live there apparently with much less inner comfort than in Russia.

No matter how you look at it, America, both in general and in particular, is a problem of Russian consciousness. Not so much a myth as a mystification. Mass attitudes of America change very fast and depend on many factors, beginning with the price rate and pay rate in Russia and finishing with the relations with our own Russian authorities. America is our "complex." It annoys, attracts, makes one think about it and compare it with the life here; it is a pure compensatory mechanism. America for Russians is not so much a political science issue as a psychoanalytical problem. It is dear to me personally as a constant source of thoughts about it.

Perhaps it has nothing to do with reality. But Russians do not care.

*Translated by Olia Prokopenko*

---

[3] A paraphrased campaign slogan of Chernomyrdin's political party.

# A Letter to Americans

## Aleksey Tsvetkov Jr.

Dear Americans: I live in a country that is almost the same as yours. There are boarding houses and ghettoes here too, supermarkets and salons, drug dealers, oligarchs and porn stars, illegal immigrants and political prisoners. Thanks for all this—if it weren't for you, I have no idea what my country would be like. Where else would we have found a role model? All sorts of Dulles plans, CIA plots, the expansion of your way of life into the East. You yourselves know better than I. Thanks to you the history of the world has temporarily stopped in conjunction with this simplification of geography, and now almost everywhere you could go on the map is The West.

I am one of those—I don't know many of them yet, but the number isn't small, even now—that is rather pleased by the similarities between our countries, even if it's the similarities between an original enterprise and a cheap imitation. In my Soviet childhood and adolescence I dreamed of being a communist in New York. I don't know if there were communists in New York at that time—somehow I never heard anything about that. Actually, no, I did. One boy from a better family and a more prestigious school told me how Angela Davis had come to his school, and, more specifically, how she wore no bra under her thin dress, and I liked that a lot. I liked New York for the glassy light of outdoor ads, Coca-Cola everywhere, crowds of drug addicts and the homeless, prostitutes on the sidewalks, rock music coming from the windows, and so forth. Only there did being a communist imply drinking Coke, reading Trotsky, listening to the Rolling Stones on headphones at McDonald's, or speaking at meetings on the steps of multistoried glossy phalluses of cellular offices.

I'm attending meetings just like that now. If the meeting spawns a conflict, we take out our homemade napalm: half soap, half bottled gasoline, and we set fire to the asphalt, repelling any invasion of the riot police that look like the cyborgs from the American cinema of my childhood. I learned this from your Black Panthers. I heard the word "napalm" for the first time in the reports on . . . Well, you guessed it already. In the film *Zabriskie Point*, which they didn't show in the Soviet Union but which I found in screenplay form in a popular Soviet magazine. I really liked the young American communist's line: "I'm prepared to contribute my car to the barricade."

Our cars were expensive, and not one communist would have agreed to part with his car, not for anything. Well, and these barricades had been relegated to history books. During my childhood, being a communist in my homeland meant: don't think, agree with everything, trample everything around you that's incomprehensible, have a stupid face. And I lamented the fact that I was not going to be made a communist, because I liked very much the general ideas, and then the dialectics. Well, unless I moved to New York. After all we didn't have drug addicts or prostitutes or homeless people or Coke or the striptease or real jeans or shiny, beautiful words like "Marlboro," a delight even if you don't smoke or have the money to. All we had were slogans, physical education over the radio, the unwieldy, outdated technology of everyday life, and bad cars. But the chances of coming to New York were slim. My mom was a yardwoman, my dad wasn't around at all, and school was unreliable: the boys who graduated went to prison, the police force, or straight to their graves; after all we had a new mafia, just like yours, and it had become fashionable to shoot each other over large amounts of money that weren't paid back punctually enough.

And the girls got married. The most beautiful to you Americans, of course. They left, and I, to this very day, can't speak English. Why bother? These days it's essentially the same here as it is there, and I can be a communist. Being a communist now means: think, agree with nothing, foster everything around you that's incomprehensible, have a profound face. Everything in its place now, thanks to your existence, your side of the globe.

But the boys in the police force, and the ones in prison, and the ones in the cemetery, and our female classmates—they all fell in love with the films of Quentin Tarantino, later on, although without catching any irony on the part of the director. It's possible, by the way, that there isn't any irony there at all, that I'm perceiving it in my typical neurotic way. All these years I've appreciated another of your directors, David Fincher. He's a real necrophiliac, in your psychoanalyst Eric Fromm's sense of the word. And I also loved Russian-American Vladimir Nabokov, who wrote about the mixing up of our two countries in his novel *Ada,* although coming from him, it looked different, ended up on a different planet. I wrote an article on Nabokov when I was in college: the *roman* of Humbert and Lolita, I argued, is like a metaphor for the *roman* of Nabokov himself and the United States. But my teachers didn't really like it. Too little literature and too much psychoanalysis.

Of course, being homeless isn't all roses, and I am in danger of becoming one of them. But for the sake of American beauty, I'm fully prepared for that and agreeable to any destiny. The dreams of my youth have come true, and it would be ordinary treachery to give them up now.

Many of the children and other relatives of once-outstanding communists from my childhood—the majority of the people in the party—have gone to live in your country. This is probably because they didn't like being the kind of communist I wanted to, and so they . . . But here I may lose my train of thought, so here I stop.

I write books in Russian which generous critics compare to your Burroughs, Hakim Bey, Chuck Palahniuk, Richard Brautigan. Russian names almost never come up in the comparisons.

I publish Russian editions of Jerry Rubin, Abby Hoffman, Hugh Houghton, Malcolm X, and other citizens of your country. I don't regret anything, although everyone in my country regrets things rather than getting out of their chairs. I don't regret anything because I'm a dialectician, not a moralist. Do I need to explain that last sentence? A dialectician sees in everything his own and the other side, trying to strengthen his own and diminish the other, while a moralist just "likes" things or "doesn't like" them.

Why should I immigrate? We have our Bukowski, Britney Spears, Charlie Manson. It's possible, by the way, that one day my country will stop being like yours, and will stop being like anything that has ever been known before, and then . . . But that wouldn't really be about America anymore.

Preachers still come from America often and distribute free Bibles and brochures. I discovered in one such brochure that "Amuru" meant "people of the West" in Biblical Hebrew, and Amerigo Vespucci, as it turns out, had almost nothing to do with it. At one time I would go to your preachers and then sell those free Bibles to vendors in the metro. If I had become a millionaire, those Bibles would have been the perfect start of my "American dream," but converting it to dollars I have about as much money now as I had then.

I only associated with a real live American on a regular basis when my wife worked for one. She went once a week to tidy up his apartment. His name was Michael, and he paid pretty well. A charming man, but not a dialectician at all. A true moralist. He hadn't even read Tom Wolfe, and Ken Kesey he only knew from films. He said he had tried Tolstoy and Dostoyevsky. Somehow I started a conversation with him about American pornography, which I like more than any other kind of pornography. Jenna Jameson, Brad Armstrong. I especially liked that they're a real family with a real family business—making and starring in pornography. I said that this was very American, that their children would be able to take over the business and make quite a profit. But Michael protested and didn't understand. He said I was still thinking of America in terms of Soviet propaganda. I said that generally in the world of pictures and ideas I prefer the antiquarian. It's really more noteworthy. Outdated propaganda has a property that becomes truth with time, but he didn't understand me, and there our conversation died. I was a real "servant of reason," or, or more precisely, husband of the servant.

What really bothers me is why when we say "America" and "American" do we always have in mind the USA and its citizens? And how do you get out of this without using the absurd "Latino"? After all they could be my Chilean friends, and my Colombian comrades, and, finally, the subcommander Marcos from Chiapas, whom I also recently published in Russian.

*Translated by Jennifer Croft*

# LOW-LEVEL FLIGHT IN TENSE ATMOSPHERIC CONDITIONS

## VLADIMIR TUCHKOV

In America, the density of matter is considerably lower than anywhere else in the world. As with every natural occurrence, this phenomenon has its positive as well as negative aspects. For the statistically-average North American, it is simpler to achieve goals than it is for a European or an African or an Asian (we won't take Australia into account because the fundamental laws there are even more whimsical). That's so because on the way to reaching a goal, the American overcomes the resistance of a rarified atmosphere, much less dense and viscose than it would be elsewhere.

At the same time, that particular property of American matter requires of an individual constant efforts aimed at "staying afloat," which is to say, maintaining his social status, not falling below a certain level, which for every category of U.S. citizenry has manufactured an industry, as Herbert Marcuse put it, of "false needs."

In connection with all this, one may compare this statistically average North American to a swimmer who must flail like a madman against very liquid water just to keep from sinking to the bottom. Or else to a bird which in the conditions of a rarified atmosphere flaps its wings with much greater frequency than would be needed under normal atmospheric circumstances.
Therefore, the healthy-lifestyle cult, so prevalent in the USA, is quite natural and completely unavoidable. Life in a rarified atmosphere demands good health. Both physical and mental.

America itself needs good health, too, because in the last decade it has found itself in roughly the same predicament as its own citizens. The Cold War has ended, and with it the standoff between the USSR and the USA. There is only one superpower left in the world. But to be a superpower and never demonstrate its superpowerness—is nonsense.

That's why the new political forces emerge in the historical arena. And this fact is not historical in nature, not political, but perfectly metaphysical. Direct and guileless, Bush knows the answer to every question. Who strives for the good of his entire nation and knows where it, this good, can be found. And is prepared to obtain it at any price.

Doubtless the terrorist attacks of September 11, 2001, were a world tragedy of the highest order. However, the crusade against terrorism that Washington has declared may lead to even more dramatic consequences, because the crusade provokes a whole number of other governments to solve their internal and external problems using the same methods that Washington does when trying, for example, to destroy the president of Iraq. In other words, the struggle against global terrorism would seem to justify any means, and does not require the consent of the UN Security Council.

Thus, for example, Russia is prepared to bomb Georgia on the basis that Tblisi does not take sufficient action against the Chechen separatists on Georgian territory—and those separatists have *very close ties to Al-Qaeda.* India is ready to start a nuclear war because Pakistan supports, not Kashmiri separatists, as they were known before, but *Islamic terrorists, trained in bin Laden's camps.* And so in international politics, the following principle is being actively introduced: If it's a *no,* but you really want it to be *yes,* then it's a *yes.*

Before, during the era of bilateralism, this sort of incident among vassals was regulated by their lords in the Kremlin and the White House. Under these new conditions, the mechanisms have not been found that would allow the world situation to stabilize. Doubtless the USA's attempts to resolve international problems by force, designating "rogue nations" that form an "axis of evil" are ineffective. The world is not nearly as simple as the current American president imagines it to be. And the coercive methods of fighting terrorism in all its forms are only a means to control the situation somewhat. This we see in the examples of Tamil and Basque separatism, and the Colombian partisan movement, which have existed for decades. At the same time, the radical leftist terrorism that was popular in Europe in the 1970s faded away because of the self-discrediting of communist ideas.

From all this it follows that the role of contemporary America on the global scene is very large indeed. And the inhabitants of this planet would like to see at the head of this superpower a more responsible administration, possessed of a better grasp of all the nuances of this particular play, written by the author unknown to us.

*Translated by Dawn L. Hannaham*

# AMERICA IN MY LIFE

## DMITRY VEDENYAPIN

The sixties: America is, for me, a child's dream of "abroad." Black-and-white as a photo which once appeared in our house. The photograph depicted a group of men (obviously Soviet) in suits and ties, against the background of an obviously foreign city: billboards, foreign cars, an elderly black man waiting by a traffic light. The third man to the left is my father. He is a translator.

I think it was from this trip that Father had brought me a toy pistol. What a beauty! We did not have anything like that for sale in our country. Naturally, I took it with me everywhere. On the fourth day of my pistol-packing excursions, I showed my pistol to another friend. An unfamiliar boy approached us. He stood still for a moment, mesmerized. Then, as if in a trance, he stretched a hand, snatched the pistol and took off. I can't say that I approved of his behavior, but I think that even then, as a seven-year-old, I understood what had happened to that boy: he had become, quite literally, *captivated by beauty.*

Another American *thing* (which remained in our possession much longer!) was the small, silvery stalagmite of the Empire State Building. My father explained to me that it was the highest building in the world. I found it particularly pleasing that the building did not have an even hundred floors, but rather—I don't remember it precisely now—a hundred two or a hundred three floors. As Leo Tolstoy said, "Art is a tiny bit of difference."

In the 1980s my friends began to leave for the U.S. A few years later, someone gave me a copy of Michael Cunningham's book *A Home at the End of the World.* I read it, and although theretofore I had only translated poetry, decided to translate prose. In the novel, the characters move in time (from the sixties to the nineties) and in space (Cleveland, New York, Phoenix, Woodstock, etc.). By the time I completed the translation, a visit to America was my greatest wish. First of all, I wanted to see whether my perception of the country was close to reality or more to my imagination. I also wanted to see close friends—émigrés, whom I did not see for many years—and to visit my sister, who was temporarily living in Manhattan, near Columbia University.

In 1999 I came to the U.S. for the first time. I arrived in New York, which simply shook me. Here are fragments from a small essay written immediately after returning to Moscow. (By the way, I understand that the black-and-white photo from my childhood was taken while strolling in Times Square.)

1. One feels that the majority of people walking on the streets have just arrived to New York themselves. Compared to crowds in Moscow, London, Stockholm, etc., who always walk slightly out of focus (as in all crowds), the New York crowd happens as if by accident (only for today are we here)—separate characters whose outlines are precisely depicted only by a contour. Everyone is on move, elastic and tightened. A multitude of bright faces.

2. In New York or by New York itself the creative task of a dichotomy is celebrated with a touch of magic: a cottage, a skyscraper, a Gothic cathedral, the glass cube of a training hall, bank, a rusty factory—all are molded next to each other, and almost reach the predictable result of a full architectural fiasco—but just when you think that the chaos has won finally and irrevocably, the city space morphs, as if by optical allusion akin to an aikido kick, into a metallic unity of rare charm.

3. In the mid-'80s I happened to visit Kiev and was struck by how that city, with its silent courtyards and rather infrequent passersby, was similar to Moscow in the '60s. In the same sense, the contemporary rhythms of Moscow and New York are on a similar wavelength.

4. New York today is like Karamzin's Paris (see *Letters of the Russian Traveler*). City of cities.

5. The rhythm of New York "substantially differs from the slow rotation of our green-blue planet" (Michael Cunningham).

As popular opinion has it, New York is full of madmen. Perhaps. But I was struck by the *normality* of its people. At the bus station I witnessed a scene which seemed to me symbolic. Two young, buff, white men, dressed in black leather and heavy chains (generally speaking, rather menacing), were unintentionally hit in their faces by a black guy's bag in the busy street traffic. My Russian experience teaches that that sort of occurrence, at best, should be followed up by an ugly argument, and, at worst—a severe fight. The Americans, however, exchanged smiling kind apologies and similarly kind assurances that these apologies were cordially accepted. Having wished each other the best of luck, these young gentlemen went on their way. I must admit that this "automatic" politeness strongly impressed me. In this country, people may wear all sorts of clothing, but in general, in certain circumstances they behave very *normally*.

In 2001 my eldest son was accepted to Harvard as a transfer student. He arrived at the university in the beginning of September. With regard to the events of 9/11, I can say only one thing: not only America, but the world as a whole became a less comfortable and fortunate place, because for a while America (it so happened) remained the last bastion of relative comfort. Today it is no longer so, which is very sad.

To end: America for me is also the English language with its active tempo-rhythm, the most logical and distinct grammar in the world, and remarkable love of precision. Let me finish with an episode from *The Magnificent Seven*: one of the seven daredevils shoots a gangster from an improbable distance, just as he is about to disappear behind the horizon. The gangster falls. "The most admirable shot I have seen in my entire life!"— exclaims a young man, and we, the spectators, together with him. "You wanted to say, the most worthless shot," the cowboy answers. "I was aiming for the horse." That's right: a shot only counts if you managed to hit what you were aiming at. The English language is a belief in the human being and his or her abilities, despite anything. It is a belief that a plan, further work, and results are connected among themselves in reality and not simply in illusion.

The fact that two of Russia's greatest "Anglo-Americans," Nabokov (in prose) and Brodsky (in poetry), made probably the greatest impression on Russian literature at the end of the twentieth century, testifies to the necessity of English-language features and qualities for Russian culture.

*Translated by Ilya Kaminsky*

# A Semester in Texas

## Andrey Zorin

## An Unexpected Situation

I spent the fall of 1996 in the south of Texas, in San Antonio, not far from the Mexican border. By this time the word "America" had already managed to lose a large part of its magic from Soviet times and was transformed into a very real country that people visit and return from. Nevertheless, even against this background, Texas, which had entered into our cultural consciousness through cowboy films and figures from jean labels of the '70s, was able to retain its aura. The state, where it is accepted practice to shoot without warning, was scary, intriguing and bewitching.

My best expectations came true almost instantly. The first thing I saw on entering the university was a notice written in bold letters, "No weapons on campus premises." Mentally approving of this wise arrangement, I went to the university library for maps and slides: I was going to be teaching local students the history of Russian civilization beginning with the invitation to the Varangians and up to the fall of communism in fourteen weeks. The documents I required were given to me on the condition that I would return them after my class because expensive materials were not allowed out of the library for more than a few hours. I was equally understanding of this foresight and was faithfully back soon after having talked about Kniaz' Vladimir and ancient Russian iconography.

The library, however, was closed and a policeman was lounging at its door.

"Someone was shot in there," he replied lazily to my natural inquisition.

"What?" I asked, deciding that I misunderstood the exotic Texas dialect, which for some reason the locals insist is close to the English of Shakespearean times.

"Someone was shot," he repeated with slight irritation and decidedly refused to explain to me what I should do with my map of Kievan Rus'.

I had to go to the Department for the right instructions.

"Shot?" the secretary asked dispassionately. "But you do not need to worry, that does not usually happen here."

"I hope," was all I could come up with as a response.

And sure enough, I was never witness to a shooting no matter how often I went to the library.

## Two Public Lectures

The program of my grant included public lectures in addition to my teaching. These lectures took place in the most unexpected of places, with the most unpredictable results.

One day I was asked to lecture—in the Russian language, which was the strictest demand of the organizers—to an army unit about the current state of affairs in Russia. From the time of the Cold War, American soldiers were given a small addition to their salaries for a certain number of semesters of Russian language at a university. The receivers of such additional pay were the ones that were sent to my lecture to improve their qualification. When I entered the auditorium, I saw about thirty young men and women, of amazing stature and beauty, looking at me with aloof attention.

Once I started speaking, I discovered very quickly that no matter how much I slowed the speed of my speech and no matter how much I simplified my lexicon and syntax, not one of the students understood one word of what I was saying. Even so, none of them turned their glance sideways, spoke to their neighbors or tried to open a book or newspaper under the table. I gave in to this military discipline and could not get up the courage to switch to English. Sweating as a result of this tortuous situation, I mumbled unintelligibly for an hour and a half into the anxiety-filled silence. In order to establish some kind of contact with the audience, I tried to say the word "El'tsin" as often as I could. Perhaps this way I was able to express at least my personal political leanings, if not the situation in Russia after the presidential elections. Anyway, the "thank you" with which I completed my talk (exactly on time), was met with loud and long applause. I don't think I ever felt that relieved in my life.

Approximately a month later I had to give a lecture—at an equivalent of a Russian Pedagogical Institute—on the unpretentious theme, "What Is Russian Literature?" Much to my surprise, a huge crowd had gathered for this talk. I have no idea what efforts it must have taken to get these people together. This time I spoke in English, thank God, and was even honored with a few questions from the audience. After the lecture, a huge, tall, red-faced person, in characteristic Texan dress—high boots and leather jacket tied together by strings—walked up to me. He held a large Texas hat in his hands.

"You know, I have read all of Dostoyevsky that has been translated into English, including his letters and diaries," he told me.

"Great," I said approvingly, not mentioning the fact that I could not boast of being so well-read myself.

"You will not believe," he continued, "I put him above Shakespeare."

"Great!" I did not object.

"But I have a problem," he complained. "I am not satisfied with what American critics write about Dostoyevsky."

"What do they write?" I was sincerely interested.

"They write that he is an existentialist. Do you agree?"

I admitted honestly that I do not agree and at his request, I named some Russian experts on Dostoyevsky whose works had been translated into English. He began to say goodbye after finding out how the names of Bakhtin and Mochulsky are transliterated.

"What do you do?" I asked him.

"I have a farm forty miles from here," he replied.

I imagined a ranch with "Problems of Dostoyevsky's Poetics" burned over the gate and thought to myself that this was the most original literary consultation I had ever given. Later, my colleagues told me that it was indeed fashionable thirty years ago to consider Dostoyevsky a predecessor of existentialists among American Slavists. Since that time several excellent works presenting other points of view have been published. It was unfortunate that I did not take the contact info of the farm-owner from San Antonio and cannot inform him about this.

## Remember the Alamo!

Ordinary Americans know about San Antonio because the Alamo is located there. The Alamo is the building of the former Catholic mission, where, during the Texas uprising of 1835, fifty-seven insurgents held off the large Mexican army, giving general Houston the chance to gather forces for a decisive battle. All of them died, but according to legend, Houston's soldiers went into battle for a free Texas with the words, "Remember the Alamo!" When, twelve years later, the state entered the United States, this American fortress became an emblem of San Antonio and one of the important relics of the heroic past of the country.

Not too long before my arrival, a Republican senator visited San Antonio. The senator was known for his age and his radical conservative views. He made a Freudian slip in his speech when he said that he was happy to be in Alamo where a handful of American lads fell in an unfair battle with 3,000 Russians.

The museum display turned out to be very predictable: old weapons and uniforms, which might have belonged to the defenders of the mission; some memoirs and a large model of the old Alamo, on which you could see how the defense took place. Several tour guides told groups of visitors about the courage of the defenders and the cruelty of the invaders. All the tour guides were Mexicans and I wanted to ask them what they actually thought about these events. However, I am sure no one would have told me anything anyway; everything was quite clear. Having established a foothold in Texas, these people got jobs and the opportunity to feed their families and give their children an education. What difference does it make now what exactly went on inside these walls more than a century and a half ago? Everything is past and forgotten.

On top of the display hung three half-raised flags. The second flag, which was swaying between the stars-and-stripes and the Texas lone-star seemed familiar to me from films I had seen, but I was not able to identify it.

"This is the Confederate flag," my companion Bridget replied with a bit of discomfort. Bridget was a professor of linguistics and had moved to Texas about fifteen years ago from Pennsylvania.

"And you can fly it with such ceremony?" I inquired.

"Well, they behave as if they won the Civil War," Bridget moved closer to whisper to me, "but that is not true, we won it."

For the first time I felt the live breath of history behind the cardboard model of the mythological narrative. And, as is always the case, the narrative itself came alive in this breath, fed by its traditional diet—the creative forgetting and poetic combining of the non-combinable.

As I found out later, the struggle for the independence of Texas was related to the prohibition of slave-ownership in Mexico. Local plantation owners heroically fought for the right to have black slaves that were nevertheless taken away from them less than thirty years later by merciless Yankees. When I found myself in the Alamo a second time, the museum looked very interesting to me.

## Children of Different Peoples

*Bapa*

Apart from the Alamo, there were four other old missions in San Antonio. At some time, Catholic monks were drawn from the relatively civilized Mexico to the wild northern forests to preach Christianity to the Indians and left these fortified temples. Now a virtual avalanche of illegal immigrants followed in their footsteps, who, in the search for a better life, wade the shallow Rio Grande by the thousands every day. These mission buildings were located in the poor Mexican districts that had a bad reputation in the city.

I was taken there by a young professor of Bengali origin, who, apart from everything else, turned out to be the grandson of Rabindranath Tagore. Bapa became favorably inclined towards me when I told him that the first English poem that I read in my life was a quatrain written by his grandpa, which was inscribed on a tin tea box that my parents ended up having (no one knows how) and that was a regular feature of the table of my childhood evenings. Apart from this reason, he saw in me a representative of another ancient culture with whom one could ironicize about barbaric America to one's heart's content.

"You will soon see the monument," he said as we approached yet another mission, "you will not believe, from the first half of the eighteenth century."

Perhaps out of a sense of false patriotism, or feeling that I was a guest, I did not explain to him that the first half of the eighteenth century is highly rated in Moscow, not to mention St. Petersburg. Anyway, I found it interesting and pleasant to talk to him.

When we reached his home, Bapa introduced me to his young wife— a student of the same university in San Antonio and the daughter of the founder of one of the main schools of Indian music, as Bapa informed me with pride. In perfect American fashion, he went off to the kitchen to take care of things while she sat and entertained me with stories of their Calcutta past.

"We were engaged when I was twelve and Bapa was nineteen," she said, smiling charmingly. "It was an arranged marriage, of course."

I thought that both my host and hostess were great candidates for life partners even without outside pressure. This made it all the more interesting to try and imagine how it must be for people whose fates were decided by others.

"You have not understood anything," said my Moscow friend, when I shared these thoughts with him. "All over the world, the offspring of kings, aristocrats and billionaires do not choose their own husbands and wives. These are not children of store-owners or university professors. In India they belonged to the high class, whereas in America they still have to try hard in order to become part of the middle class. So they are proud about their dynastic wedding because they are nostalgic about their lost status."

I was ashamed. I had studied noble culture for so long but failed to understand such a simple thing. Apparently the stereotypes, fostered by the clichés of petty bourgeois literature, proved themselves to be too steadfast.

*Humbert*

The person who bore the name of the hero in *Lolita* was the husband of the Russian-language instructor. Her last name, Rouble, would also have been perfectly appropriate for a colleague from any of Nabokov's American novels. Humbert received his law degree in Germany, worked in San Antonio as a bartender and had a phenomenal collection of alcoholic drinks. Having found out from his wife about my visit, he considered it his duty to treat me to Russian vodka.

We talked a little about German soccer, remembered Mueller, Beckenbauer and Mattheus, complained a bit that Americans do not understand anything about this wonderful sport. After yet another shot—we had lost count of them—it was time for international friendship and my host asked me if anyone in my family had suffered as a result of the war. I did not deny the obvious and did not hide the fact that it was hardly possible to find a single family in Russia where someone had not suffered as a result of the war. After hearing this simple information, Humbert started crying most naturally and started talking about his grandfather for whom the years spent during World War I as a POW in the Ukraine were the best time in his life.

"It's the same with Texas," he explained to me. "Germans love the land, but they do not have any and when they see a lot of land, they are very happy."

The pining of the lawyer, re-trained as a bartender, for the Lebensraum should have served as a warning to me. But I was touched and completely ready for drunken hugs. Soon, however, I was shocked to hear something totally unexpected.

"We were set off against each other," said Humbert, "but we should have been together. We would have showed them then."

"Who 'them'?" I asked, stunned.

"Them," he said, pointing in the general direction of his wife, "the Americans, the British and the French. They think they are the masters of the world, but the world should belong to us Germans and Russians."

"I am a Jew," I said, solely with the aim of breaking up this intended Molotov-Ribbentrop pact.

"All the better," said Humbert decisively.

I did not try to find out the reason for which this was all the better. My head was ringing and I could not clearly understand what I was seeing: the sudden breaking out on the surface of family complexes or geopolitical paranoia. It is very possible that these are one and the same thing.

### Farewell to Arms

I was reminiscing about my origins sooner than I expected. Before Thanksgiving Day I left San Antonio for a short time, and on returning I went straight to the Department office where I discovered several notes in my mailbox. Looking them over, I found out that several people whom I did not know had left me their phone numbers. The secretary was not able to explain anything to me but said that she had tried her best to note down all the calls she had received.

I decided to deal with this telephone avalanche at home, but I had hardly opened the door and put my bag down when the telephone rang.

"Andrew," a jubilant voice roared into the telephone. "This is your uncle Bob."

I have no idea just how many question marks would be required to express the intonation of my answer. Be that as it may, in the course of further conversation I partly found out and partly remembered the family story about how my grandfather's sister left Odessa for New York through Paris, in 1914, just before the war. It turned out that their correspondence continued for exactly twenty years and, as a consequence, I later had a chance to see dozens of letters from my grandfather and photographs I had never seen before, of my grandmother and my dad. Their correspondence was cut short in 1934: either the letters stopped reaching the recipients, or they themselves stopped writing to each other. Both were equally valid possibilities. Our American relatives started looking for us in the mid-fifties. They had very little doubt that none of us were alive. One of my cousins told me later that they basically wanted to find out whether it was Hitler or Stalin that was responsible for the demise of the Russian branch of the family.

Their persistence paid off just like in a moralistic novella. After forty years and God knows how many attempts, the Red Cross located my father, who gave them my telephone numbers in Texas. Of course, my cousin's grandmother had passed on in this time, but one of her children and three grandsons were alive and unbelievably happy that their efforts succeeded beyond any expectation. After three hours I had spoken with all of them.

After a couple of weeks and right before my final departure from America, one of my newly acquired cousins twice-removed flew into San Antonio to meet with me. He spent four years as a Marine and then trained as a hotel manager in Las Vegas. He turned out to be very warm and nice, but a very shy and quiet young man. Probably to avoid speaking too much about himself, he turned the conversation around to the comparative merits of American and Soviet arms. I found out that the Kalashnikov was better than its American analog but our Armored Vehicle Carriers were no good and it was incomprehensible how it was feasible to fight in them.

Unfortunately, my own life experience did not give me sufficient ability to keep up this conversation. However, I did note to myself that the theme of arms, which kicked off my Texas visit, was, according to the law of cyclical composition, recalled towards its end.

On the day after Justin flew back to Nevada, the Department organized a farewell dinner in my honor. Still under the impression of recent events, I told my colleagues about my family history. In response I heard an even more fascinating story from one of our professors.

He was brought here from Poland when he was just three. His parents were extremely religious Catholics and raised their son accordingly. However, it looks like they overdid the religious part a bit. Tired of Sunday Mass, he discovered at a young age that most of his friends were Jews. Later he got married to one, and even though his wife was not overly religious, he converted to Judaism. Naturally, this conversion did not please his parents, but they reconciled to it and accepted his wife. After twenty years his mother died and he, along with his adopted black daughter, flew to her funeral. Only then, looking at his family archives, he discovered that his parents were Jews as well. Perhaps what happened to them in Poland during the occupation scared them so much that they were too afraid to tell their son the truth even after he chose for himself a Jewish life.

To be honest, I do not believe much in ethnic mystique and the call of blood. People build their own individual mythologies according to the same rules that nations use. It is possible that my interlocutor sensed something amiss in his childhood, and the forbidden synagogue became a desired alternative to the enforced experience of the Catholic cathedral. It is possible, too, that his spiritual evolution had some other reasons as well. The most interesting thing for me in this story was his black daughter. What a combination of Jewish, Catholic, African-American, American, and Texas traditions she would have to forge the mosaic of her self-identity from! My flight landed in a snow-covered Sheremet'evo and I was still trying to figure out this combustible mix.

When I tell my friends in different American universities that I fell in love with Texas, they are surprised and ask me the reason why.

Have I been able to explain?

*Translated by Susmita Sundaram*

# CONTRIBUTORS

## AUTHORS

**Mikhail Aizenberg** is a poet and works as a journalist for various Moscow magazines writing on contemporary Russian poetry. He was born in 1948 in Moscow, where he graduated from the Moscow Institute of Architecture. He is the author of a collection of essays *A Look at a Free Artist* (1997), as well as the poetry collections *Index of Names* (1993), *Punctuation of a Place* (1995), *Beyond the Red Gate* (2000), and *Other and Previous Works* (2001). An issue of *Russian Studies in Literature* (Spring 1996) featured translations of his work.

**Anatoly Barzakh** is a literary critic who was born in 1950. He graduated from Leningrad State University, where he received a doctorate in physics and mathematics. He is a senior staff member at the Petersburg Institute of Nuclear Physics and the editor of *Academic Project*. He has published articles and essays about the poetry of Annenski, Mandelshtam, Ivanov, Kushner, Dragomoschenko and others for magazines including *Postcriptum, Commentaries,* and *New Russian Book*. His books include *A Feeling of Heaviness* (about Mandelshtam's poem "He Who Found a Horseshoe") as well as the essay compilation *A Reverse Translation*. He lives in St. Petersburg.

**Dmitry Bavilsky** is a critic, prose writer, and poet. He was born in 1969 in Chelyabinsk in the Urals. He graduated from the philological department of Chelyabinsk University. He published two books of poems, three novels, a collection of stories, some plays, and more than 500 articles about contemporary literature in major newspapers and magazines throughout Russia. He was the deputy editor of the magazine *Ural Novelty* from 1995 to 1999. For the past several years he has written for the literary magazine *Topos*. He has sat on the jury for a number of literature awards, and he is a member of the Academy of Contemporary Russian Literature.

**Marina Boroditskaya** is a poet and translator. She was born in 1954 in Moscow, where she graduated in 1976 from the Moscow State Institute of Foreign Languages. She is well known as a translator of English, American, and French classical poetry, including Chaucer (the first Russian translation of *Troilus and Criseyde*), Donne, Burns, Keats, Kipling, Longfellow, etc. She is the author of three books of verse—*I'm Undressing a Soldier* (1994), *Single Skating* (1999), *The Year of Horse* (2002)—and more than a dozen books for children. Her work has been appearing in "thick monthlies" like *Novy Mir* and *Foreign Literature* regularly since 1978. She also conducts a "Radio Russia" program called "Literary Pharmacy," contributes columns to the BBC radio service, and works as a freelance interpreter at international events.

**Evgeny Bunimovich** is a poet. He was born in 1954. He graduated from the Moscow State University department of mathematics. He is an honored teacher of the Russian Federation and vice-president of the Association of Teachers of Mathematics. Since the 1990s he has been active in politics and a member of the political council of the party "Apple." He is a deputy to the Moscow City Duma, for which he supervises city education and culture. He is a founder of the Moscow club "Poetry." He has participated in international poetry festivals and proposed the idea for the Moscow International Festival of Poets, for which he serves as chairman. He is also editor of the anthology *Les poetes de la nouvelle vague en Russie* published in 1994 in Belgium. His first book was published in 1990 and his selected poems, *Natural Selection*, was printed in two editions in 2000-2001. His verses have been published in France, Belgium, Sweden, Israel, Germany, and the USA.

**Oleg Dark** is a prose writer and literary critic, born in 1959. He graduated from the Moscow State University department of philology where he wrote his thesis on Dostoevsky. From 1981 to 1982 he was a research assistant in the Pushkin Museum. He has a degree in International Education specializing in Methodology. He worked in the Regional House of Pioneers. From 1985 to 1987 he worked as a janitor at an institute of blood transfusion and an institute of hydromechanics. He is the author of the story collection *Trilogy* (1996); of articles, stories, and essays which were published in the publications *Friendship of Nations, Banner, Questions of Literature, New Literary View, Brook, Archer, A Messenger of New Russian Literature, Independent Newspaper, Literary Newspaper, General Newspaer,* and others. He has written commentaries on the work of Sologub, Nabokov, and Rozanov. He assembled three volumes of *Selected Prose of Russians Abroad* (2000). He is married and has two children.

Arkadii Dragomoschenko is a poet and prose writer. He was born in 1946 and studied philology and theory of theatre in different universities. He has been a recipient of numerous Russian and international literary awards. Several of his books of poetry (such as *Description* and *Xenia*) and prose (*Phosphor* and *Under Suspicion*) have been translated into other languages, including English. He is a noted translator of American poetry and a literary-magazine editor, and he has taught at St. Petersburg University, University of California (San Diego), and SUNY (Buffalo). He lives in St. Petersburg. "Do Not a Gun" is excerpted from Dragomoschenko's latest book *Dust.*

Max Frai is a prose and fiction writer as well as a publicist. He is the author of a number of literary projects including a cycle of science fiction best-sellers, a collection of essays about literature and art, the reference book *The ABCs of Contemporary Art* and literary anthologies on classical writers of world literature and contemporary Russian authors (*A Book of Indecencies, A Book of Fantasy Worlds, Russian Heterogeneous Fairy Tale*, and others). He supervises the book series *From the Books of Max Frai*, which is published by Amfora (St. Petersburg). He is also the pen-name belonging to artist Svetlana Martynchik, a Russian artist of Ukrainian origin, born in 1965 in Odessa and living now in Moscow.

Maria Galina is a poet and prose writer born in 1958. She graduated from the biology department at Odessa University. She holds a doctorate in biological sciences and specializes in marine biology. She published two books of poems and three books of prose (her novel, *A Blanket for Avaddon*, made the shortlist for the Appolon Grigorev Award in 2000). For several years she was a literary reviewer for *Literary Newspaper*, specializing in modern science fiction and poetry.

Sergey Gandlevsky is a poet and prose writer. He was born in 1952, graduated from the philology department at Moscow University. An underground poet during the Soviet 1970s and '80s, he is the winner of both the Little Booker Prize and the Anti-Booker Prize in 1996 for his poetry and prose. He is the author of four books of poems; a memoir, *Trepanation of the Skull* (1996); a book of essays, *Poetic Cuisine* (1998); and a novel *{Unintel.}* (2001). He has been included in English translation anthologies *20th Century Russian Poetry: Silver and Steel* (Doubleday Press, 1993), *The Third Wave* (University of Michigan Press, 1992), and *In the Grip of Strange Thoughts: Russian Poetry in a New Era* (Zephyr Press 1999). *A Kindred Orphanhood: Selected Poems of Sergey Gandlevsky*, translated by Philip Metres, was published by Zephyr Press in October 2003.

**Linor Goralik** is a writer and journalist living and working in Russia. She was born in the Ukraine in 1975 and immigrated to Israel in 1989. In the year 2000 she returned to Russia to live in Moscow. A graduate of the computer science department at Beer-Sheva University, she recently left the hi-tech industry to concentrate solely on writing. Her prose has been published in a number of journals and anthologies, and three books of her own (one written in cooperation with Sergey Kuznetsov) are forthcoming.

**Olga Ilnitskaya** was born not far from Odessa. She has a degree in history and the social sciences. She graduated from Odessa State University. She has worked as a teacher of history, a guide, a research assistant, a janitor, an archivist, and a correspondent. She has lived in Moscow since 2001. She has published two books of poems and prose. Her texts were published in magazines and anthologies such as *Neva, Youth, Scratchpaper* (New York), *Honeycomb* (Kiev), *Archer* (Moscow) and others.

**Leonid Kostyukov** is a poet, prose writer and literary critic. He was born in 1959. He graduated from the department of mechanics and mathematics at Moscow State University and the Literary Institute, where he took seminars with Anatoly Kim. He taught literature and math in school. His articles, essays, poems, and prose have appeared in *Friendship of Nations, Weekly Magazine, Independent Newspaper, Week, Pushkin, Russian Telegraph, Postscriptum, Solo,* and others. He also published a book of stories called *He Returned to Our City* and the novel *Great Country*. He won the literary competition "Catch" in spring 2000. He is a father of three children.

**Grigori Kruzhkov** is a poet and translator, born in 1945. He graduated from the physics department of Tomsk University and attended graduate school specializing in the physics of high energies. He published poems and translations of foreign poetry, mainly from English, starting with John Donne and ending with William Yeats. He is an author of four books of poems. He also wrote and translated poetry for children. He assembled a volume of research in the history of Russian poetry of the Silver Age and Russian-English literary connections. He taught at Columbia University and now lives in Moscow.

**Artur Kudashev** is a prose writer, born in 1967. He graduated from Bashkir Medical Institute in psychiatry. His works were published in the literary periodicals of Bashkiria. Some of his stories were included in the anthology *Literature Not from the Capital* (2002). He lives in Ufa.

**Dmitry Kuzmin** is a poet, translator, critic, and literary organizer. He was born in 1968. He graduated from the Moscow Pedagogical University in the department of philology. He is the chief editor of ARGO-RISK, which specializes in publishing modern Russian literature, poetry in particular. In 1989 he co-founded Babylon, the union of young writers. He is an organizer of a number of literary festivals and a supervisor of the Internet anthology of modern Russian literature (www.vavilon.ru). He has translated American poetry and French prose into Russian. His poems have been published in the USA, England, France, Italy, and Poland.

**Aleksandr Levin** was born in 1957. He graduated from the Moscow Institute of Transport Engineers where he specialized in computer engineering. He is an author of one of the most popular Russian textbooks for beginning computer users. He is also the author of two books of verse and two albums of songs written and performed by him.

**Sergey Leybgrad** is a poet, culturologist, and publicist. He was born in Kuybyshev (which is today Samara) in 1962. He graduated from the department of culturology at the Samara Art and Culture Institute. His verses and essays about contemporary arts were published in magazines and anthologies such as *Island* (Berlin), *An Hour of Culture* (Poland), *Pushkin, Russian Magazine, Golden Century, New Literary Review, Friendship of Nations, Performance,* and others. He is the author of seven books of poems. He is an organizer of international festivals of factual arts in Samara and Tolyatti such as European Days in

Samara (1996-98), Pushkin After Pushkin (1999), Theater as a Text, Dialog Without Mediators (2000-02), and others. From 1995 to 1998 he served as chief of *Circus Olymp*, a monthly review of literature and arts. Currently he is an author and a host of several TV programs in Samara.

**Stanislav Lvovsky** is a poet and prose writer. He was born in 1972. He lives in Moscow. He graduated from the chemistry department at Moscow State University. He taught chemistry and English in high school. Currently he works in advertising and public relations. He is the author of the poetry collection *White Noise* (1996), the prose collection *The Word on Flowers and Dogs* (2003), and a mixed collection of poetry, prose, and translations, *Three Months of the Year 02* (2002). He translated American poetry of the twentieth century (Charles Bukowski, Charles Reznikoff, and others). He designs books for the publisher ARGO-RISK. In 1989 he co-founded Babylon, the union of young writers. He is laureate of the Fourth Festival of Free Verse in Moscow in 1993. He is a three-time laureate of the literary competition "Snare." He is a member of the board of editors of the literary journal *TextOnly*.

**Aleksey Mikheev** is a prose writer born in 1953. He graduated from the economics department at Moscow State University in 1974. He defended a dissertation in psycholinguistics in 1984. He was the host of a literary program on the radio channel *Echo of Moscow* from 1994 to 1995. From 1995 to 2002 he worked for the magazine *Foreign Literature*. He is coauthor of the book *Meaning and Categorization* (New York, 1996). He is the author of the prose book *A and B Sat on a Chimney*.

**Dmitry Prigov** was born in Moscow, in 1940, and has lived there all his life. He was trained as an artist at the Stroganov Art Institute, from which he was expelled during Khrushchev's attack on Formalist and Abstractionist artists. He was reinstated a year later and graduated in 1967. He began writing poetry in 1957. Prigov collects his poems in cycles, each one containing twenty poems, arranged in the manner of samizdat. So far he has produced more than 150 such "books" or about 24,000 poems. Since the early 1970s, he has been creating visual and manipulative texts, mini-books (texts inscribed on cans), window-texts and telegrams.

**Igor Shevelev** is a prose writer and a critic, born in 1952. He graduated from the philosophy department at Moscow State University. Since 1987 he has worked in the field of journalism and literary criticism. He has published many articles, reviews, and interviews in the newspapers *Moscow News, New Russian Word, Common Newspaper, Independent Newspaper*, and others. He has also published two novels.

**Aleksey Tsvetkov Jr.** is a prose writer. He was born in 1975. He graduated from the Literature Institute in Moscow. For many years he was the leader of the student unions "Defense" and "Purple International" and other radical socio-political organizations. He served as a secretary for the newspaper of the national Bolshevik party "Limonka." He is the curator of the Internet project www.anarh.ru, and his political and cultural essays are included in the framework of this project. He is the author of three books of prose and a book of radical left political journalism. He lives in Moscow.

**Vladimir Tuchkov** is a poet and prose writer, born in 1949. He graduated from the Moscow Forestry Technology Institute. He worked as a computer programmer and diagram technician. In 1990 he started working in journalism. He is a laureate of the Turgenev Festival of Short Prose. He was awarded cash prizes for his writing from the magazines *New World* and *Zhvanetsky's Store*. He is the author of four books of prose.

**Dmitry Vedenyapin** was born in 1959 in Moscow. He is the author of two collections of verses, *Cover* (1993) and *The Grass and a Smoke* (2002), and numerous translations.

**Andrey Zorin** was born in 1956. He is Associate Professor of Russian Literature at the Russian State University for the Humanities. He received a Ph.D. (kandidatskaia) from Moscow State University in 1983 for his dissertation "The Literature of Sensibility In England and Russia." Since the late 1980s, he has taught as a visiting professor at Harvard, Stanford, University of Helsinki, University of Texas (Austin), and L'Ecole des Hautes Etudes en Sciences Sociales (Paris). He is the author of more than one hundred articles and reviews dealing with the subject of Russian literature, culture and ideology of the eighteenth and nineteenth centuries as well as contemporary Russian culture.

## TRANSLATORS

**Jennifer Croft** holds an MFA in Translation from the University of Iowa and has translated Russian, Polish, and Bosnian authors. She lives in Warsaw.

**Thomas Epstein** is a writer and translator who teaches Russian and Comparative Literature at Boston College.

**Andrea Gregovich** studied English and Russian studies at DePauw University and has spent time in Ukraine, Croatia, and Russia. She currently lives in Las Vegas, where she's working on her novel *Martyred Cars* in the Master of Fine Arts program at the University of Nevada.

**Dawn L. Hannaham** is a writer, poet, translator, editor, jewelry designer, and occasional performance artist. She writes in English, Russian, Spanish, and French. In 2001, one of her poems was read at the transfer ceremony for "Zvezda," a nuclear waste processing and storage facility in the Russian Far East. She is currently studying classical Arabic.

**Ilya Kaminsky's** book of poems, *Dancing in Odessa*, is the recent winner of Tupelo Press's Dorset Prize. He is also the winner of *Poetry's* Ruth Lilly Fellowship and of Milton Center's Award for Excellence in Literature. His work appears or is forthcoming in *The New Republic, Southwest Review, Salmagundi, Doubletake, American Literary Review* and many other publications.

**J. Kates** is a poet and literary translator. He is co-director of Zephyr Press and editor of *In the Grip of Strange Thoughts: Russian Poetry in a New Era.*

**Katya Kumkova-Wolpert** has been dealing in language and cultural concepts since 1991, when she moved with her family from St. Petersburg, Russia to Oshkosh, WI. She has worked on various translation projects, produced news from the U.S. for Moscow television and has recently moved to Germany. She is considering translating Wladimer Kaminer's *Russendisko* into English.

**Philip Metres**'s poems and translations have appeared in numerous journals and in the anthologies *Best American Poetry* (2002) and *In the Grip of Strange Thoughts: Russian Poetry in a New Era* (Zephyr, 1999). *A Kindred Orphanhood: Selected Poems of Sergey Gandlevsky* is forthcoming from Zephyr Press (Fall 2003). *Catalogue of Comedic Novelties: Selected Poems of Lev Rubinstein*, a collaboration with Tatiana Tulchinsky, is forthcoming from Ugly Duckling Presse (Fall 2003). *Primer for Non-Native Speakers*, a chapbook, is forthcoming from Wick Poetry Series (Kent State, 2004). He works as an assistant professor of English at John Carroll University, living in Cleveland, Ohio.

**Julia Mikhailova** was born in Krasnoyarsk in Siberia. She teaches Russian at the Middlebury Summer Language School and at The Ohio State University, where she is a doctoral candidate in Slavic linguistics. She has degrees in philology from Krasnoyarsk State Pedagogical University and Syracuse University.

**Olia Prokopenko** was born in Kharkiv, Ukraine. She graduated from Karazin National University, Kharkiv (English Language and Literature; French Language and Literature). She received a Ph.D. (Aspirantura) in Comparative Linguistics at Skovoroda Pedagogical University, Kharkiv. She has taught at Skovoroda Pedagogical University, Lafayette College (Pennsylvania), and The Ohio State University.

**Yelizaveta P. Renfro** is in the MFA program at George Mason University, where she was named the Heritage Writer for 2003-04. Her work is forthcoming in *Glimmer Train Stories* and *The North American Review*. She was born in the Soviet Union to a Russian mother and American father, came to the U.S. at the age of three, and grew up in a bilingual household in Riverside, California. Currently she lives in Herndon, Virginia.

**Susmita Sundaram** is currently completing her dissertation on Konstantin Bal'mont. She lived in Moscow from 1994 to 1998.

**Efrem Yankelevich** was active in the Soviet human rights movement until he was pressured to leave the USSR. In Europe and in the U.S., he continued to campaign for the release of prisoners of conscience. He is currently writing a book on the historical basis of the Soviet social system.

**Matvei Yankelevich**'s English translations of Daniil Kharms have appeared in *3rd Bed*, *New American Writing*, *Open City*, and other magazines. He is currently co-translating an anthology of Oberiu writers to be published by Northwestern University Press. Matvei co-edits *6x6,* a poetry periodical, and is series editor of the new Eastern European Poets Series from the small Brooklyn publishing collective, Ugly Duckling Presse.

## About the Editors

**Mikhail Iossel** is a native of St. Petersburg, Russia, where he worked as an engineer, a boiler-room operator, and a night guard. Since 1986 he has lived in the U.S. and has an MFA in English (creative writing) from the University of New Hampshire. He was a Stegner Fellow in creative writing at Stanford University from 1989 to '91. His short stories have been published in a number of literary magazines and anthologized in the *Best American Short Stories,* among other places. He has also been published in *samizdat* magazines and is the author of the collection of stories *Every Hunter Wants to Know* (W.W. Norton, 1991). He has been a recipient of Guggenheim Foundation and NEA fellowships. Since 1995, he has been a writer-in-residence at Union College. He is the Founder and Director of the Summer Literary Seminars program (www.sumlitsem.org).

**Jeff Parker**'s fiction, nonfiction, and hypertext have appeared in *Ploughshares*, *Tin House*, *The Iowa Review*, *The Mississippii Review*, and others. He has written about contemporary Russian literature, music, and culture for such publications as *Poets & Writers*, *Spin* magazine, and *Billiards Digest*. He has been involved in the Summer Literary Seminars program in St. Petersburg, Russia, since 1999 and is currently the Co-Director.

## Acknowledgments

The editors wish to thank the Moscow poet and literary organizer Dmitry Kuzmin for his efforts in making this anthology possible. His endeavors as a promoter of the literary arts in Russia are of tremendous importance. Without him this anthology could not be.

# SELECTED DALKEY ARCHIVE PAPERBACKS

# FOR A FULL LIST OF PUBLICATIONS, VISIT:
# www.dalkeyarchive.com

Carleton College Library
One North College Street
Northfield, MN 55057-4097

# SELECTED DALKEY ARCHIVE PAPERBACKS

*Springer's Progress.*
*Wittgenstein's Mistress.*
CAROLE MASO, *AVA.*
LADISLAV MATEJKA AND KRYSTYNA POMORSKA, EDS.,
  *Readings in Russian Poetics: Formalist and Structuralist*
  *Views.*
HARRY MATHEWS,
  *The Case of the Persevering Maltese: Collected Essays.*
  *Cigarettes.*
  *The Conversions.*
  *The Human Country: New and Collected Stories.*
  *The Journalist.*
  *Singular Pleasures.*
  *The Sinking of the Odradek Stadium.*
  *Tlooth.*
  *20 Lines a Day.*
ROBERT L. MCLAUGHLIN, ED.,
  *Innovations: An Anthology of Modern &*
    *Contemporary Fiction.*
STEVEN MILLHAUSER, *The Barnum Museum.*
  *In the Penny Arcade.*
RALPH J. MILLS, JR., *Essays on Poetry.*
OLIVE MOORE, *Spleen.*
NICHOLAS MOSLEY, *Accident.*
  *Assassins.*
  *Catastrophe Practice.*
  *Children of Darkness and Light.*
  *The Hesperides Tree.*
  *Hopeful Monsters.*
  *Imago Bird.*
  *Impossible Object.*
  *Inventing God.*
  *Judith.*
  *Natalie Natalia.*
  *Serpent.*
  *The Uses of Slime Mould: Essays of Four Decades.*
WARREN F. MOTTE, JR.,
  *Fables of the Novel: French Fiction since 1990.*
  *Oulipo: A Primer of Potential Literature.*
YVES NAVARRE, *Our Share of Time.*
WILFRIDO D. NOLLEDO, *But for the Lovers.*
FLANN O'BRIEN, *At Swim-Two-Birds.*
  *At War.*
  *The Best of Myles.*
  *The Dalkey Archive.*
  *Further Cuttings.*
  *The Hard Life.*
  *The Poor Mouth.*
  *The Third Policeman.*
CLAUDE OLLIER, *The Mise-en-Scène.*
FERNANDO DEL PASO, *Palinuro of Mexico.*
ROBERT PINGET, *The Inquisitory.*
RAYMOND QUENEAU, *The Last Days.*
  *Odile.*
  *Pierrot Mon Ami.*
  *Saint Glinglin.*
ANN QUIN, *Berg.*
  *Passages.*
  *Three.*
  *Tripticks.*
ISHMAEL REED, *The Free-Lance Pallbearers.*
  *The Last Days of Louisiana Red.*
  *Reckless Eyeballing.*
  *Threes.*
  *Twos.*

*Yellow Back Radio Broke-Down.*
JULIÁN RÍOS, *Poundemonium.*
AUGUSTO ROA BASTOS, *I the Supreme.*
JACQUES ROUBAUD, *The Great Fire of London.*
  *Hortense in Exile.*
  *Hortense Is Abducted.*
  *The Plurality of Worlds of Lewis.*
  *The Princess Hoppy.*
  *Some Thing Black.*
LEON S. ROUDIEZ, *French Fiction Revisited.*
LUIS RAFAEL SÁNCHEZ, *Macho Camacho's Beat.*
SEVERO SARDUY, *Cobra & Maitreya.*
NATHALIE SARRAUTE, *Do You Hear Them?*
  *Martereau.*
ARNO SCHMIDT, *Collected Stories.*
  *Nobodaddy's Children.*
CHRISTINE SCHUTT, *Nightwork.*
GAIL SCOTT, *My Paris.*
JUNE AKERS SEESE,
  *Is This What Other Women Feel Too?*
  *What Waiting Really Means.*
AURELIE SHEEHAN, *Jack Kerouac Is Pregnant.*
VIKTOR SHKLOVSKY,
  *A Sentimental Journey: Memoirs 1917-1922.*
  *Theory of Prose.*
  *Third Factory.*
  *Zoo, or Letters Not about Love.*
JOSEF ŠKVORECKÝ,
  *The Engineer of Human Souls.*
CLAUDE SIMON, *The Invitation.*
GILBERT SORRENTINO, *Aberration of Starlight.*
  *Blue Pastoral.*
  *Crystal Vision.*
  *Imaginative Qualities of Actual Things.*
  *Mulligan Stew.*
  *Pack of Lies.*
  *The Sky Changes.*
  *Something Said.*
  *Splendide-Hôtel.*
  *Steelwork.*
  *Under the Shadow.*
W. M. SPACKMAN, *The Complete Fiction.*
GERTRUDE STEIN, *Lucy Church Amiably.*
  *The Making of Americans.*
  *A Novel of Thank You.*
PIOTR SZEWC, *Annihilation.*
ESTHER TUSQUETS, *Stranded.*
DUBRAVKA UGRESIC, *Thank You for Not Reading.*
LUISA VALENZUELA, *He Who Searches.*
BORIS VIAN, *Heartsnatcher.*
PAUL WEST, *Words for a Deaf Daughter & Gala.*
CURTIS WHITE, *Memories of My Father Watching TV.*
  *Monstrous Possibility.*
  *Requiem.*
DIANE WILLIAMS, *Excitability: Selected Stories.*
  *Romancer Erector.*
DOUGLAS WOOLF, *Wall to Wall.*
  *Ya! & John-Juan.*
PHILIP WYLIE, *Generation of Vipers.*
MARGUERITE YOUNG, *Angel in the Forest.*
  *Miss MacIntosh, My Darling.*
REYOUNG, *Unbabbling.*
LOUIS ZUKOFSKY, *Collected Fiction.*
SCOTT ZWIREN, *God Head.*

FULL LIST OF PUBLICATIONS, VISIT:
www.dalkeyarchive.com